Cambridge IGCSE®

Mandarin Chinese

Yan Burch

HODDER EDUCATION
AN HACHETTE UK COMPANY

®IGCSE is the registered trademark of Cambridge International Examinations.

All questions and answers are written by the author.

Answers can be found at www.hoddereducation.com/cambridgeextras

Every effort has been made to trace all copyright holders, but if any have been inadvertently overlooked the publishers will be pleased to make the necessary arrangements at the first opportunity.

Although every effort has been made to ensure that website addresses are correct at time of going to press, Hodder Education cannot be held responsible for the content of any website mentioned in this book. It is sometimes possible to find a relocated web page by typing in the address of the home page for a website in the URL window of your browser.

Hachette UK's policy is to use papers that are natural, renewable and recyclable products and made from wood grown in sustainable forests. The logging and manufacturing processes are expected to conform to the environmental regulations of the country of origin.

Orders: please contact Bookpoint Ltd, 130 Milton Park, Abingdon, Oxon OX14 4SB.
Telephone: (44) 01235 827720. Fax: (44) 01235 400454. Email education@bookpoint.co.uk
Lines are open 9.00–5.00, Monday to Saturday, with a 24-hour message answering service.

Visit our website at www.hoddereducation.com.

First published in 2017 by

Hodder Education

An Hachette UK Company

Carmelite House, 50 Victoria Embankment, London EC4Y 0DZ

Impression number 5 4 3 2 1

Year 2019 2018 2017

Cover photo © Digifoto Gamma / Alamy

This edition typeset in Graphicraft Limited, Hong Kong

Printed in Slovenia

A catalogue record for this title is available from the British Library

9781471890253

目录

第四单元 高校与工作

附录

Contents

Unit 4 Further education and the world of work

Introduction

How to use this book

This book is suitable for learners with an elementary knowledge of Chinese or those that have studied Chinese for one to two years. It can be used as a supplementary resource for independent study or as a classroom text book for students taking the Cambridge ICGSE® Mandarin Chinese course.

This book contains all topic areas from the course specification as well as all the minimum core vocabulary, and the full range of sentence structures as specified within the 2017 Defined Content on the Cambridge International Examinations website.

Every unit starts with an opening page of warm-up activities and ends with a 'Did you know …' section which not only provides cultural information but can also serve as extended reading practice.

Each chapter covers all fours skills: speaking, listening, reading and writing. This is complemented by exam-style exercises with specified rubrics. Pinyin (phonetics) is given in the speaking section. Grammar is explained clearly in plain language and is backed up with comprehensive example sentences.

The level of content and exercises is arranged progressively from simple, to complex and comprehensive. Rubrics are given in both English and Chinese, so students have the opportunity to absorb the information in both languages. Throughout the book, there are tips to help with study.

A full range of complementary resources including transcripts for listening materials, answers and translations of the practice texts can be found at www.hoddereducation.com/cambridgeextras

Icon guide

These icons are used throughout the book to signpost the different skills.

Tip

Reading

Listening

Vocabulary

Grammar

Speaking

Writing

As you read through the book, you will notice some green shaded area in the text. The green shaded vocabulary goes beyond the Cambridge IGCSE® minimum core vocabulary list. Activities shaded green can be used as extension activities.

Introductions and greetings

nǐ hǎo 你好！	Hello!
wǒ lái jiè shào yí xià zhè wèi shì 我来介绍一下，这位是……	Let me introduce, this is …
rèn shi nǐ wǒ hěn gāo xìng 认识你我很高兴！	Nice to meet you!
zhè shì wǒ de míng piàn 这是我的名片。	This is my card.
nǐ hǎo ma 你好吗？	How are you?
wǒ hěn hǎo xiè xie 我很好，谢谢！	I am very well, thank you!
qǐng wèn 请问，……	Please, may I ask … / Excuse me, …
zài jiàn 再见！	Goodbye! / See you again!
hǎo jiǔ bú jiàn le 好久不见了！	Long time no see!
zhù nǐ shēng rì kuài lè 祝你生日快乐！	Happy birthday to you!
néng má fan nǐ yí xià ma 能麻烦你一下吗？	May I trouble you?
xiè xie nín de bāng zhù 谢谢您的帮助！	Thank you for your help!
bú xiè 不谢！	Don't mention it!
tài má fan nǐ le 太麻烦你了！	Sorry for the trouble!
bú kè qì 不客气！	You are welcome! / No need to be so polite!
qǐng yuán liàng duì bù qǐ 请原谅！/对不起！	Please pardon me! / I am sorry!
méi guān xi 没关系！	It doesn't matter!

1

第一单元 个人与社交

Unit 1 Personal and social life

你是哪国人？ Which country are you from?

1 Match each country to the correct flag.

dé guó 德国	fǎ guó 法国	mǎ lái xī yà 马来西亚	rì běn 日本	xīn jiā pō 新加坡	yìn dù 印度	yìn ní 印尼	měi guó 美国	zhōng guó 中国

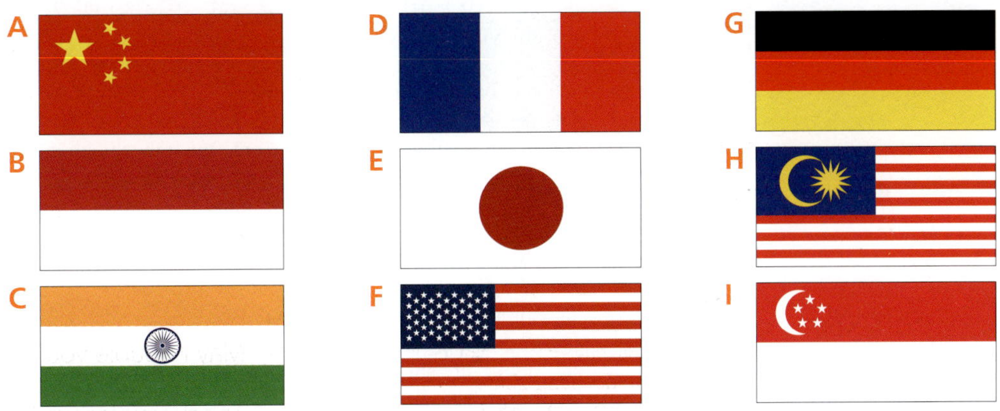

2 Here is a map of the world. Give the name of each continent in both Chinese and English.

ào zhōu 澳洲 Australia	fēi zhōu 非洲 Africa	měi zhōu 美洲 America	ōu zhōu 欧洲 Europe	yà zhōu 亚洲 Asia	nán jí zhōu 南极洲 Antarctica

第一章 我和家人

Dialogue A

小明 and 玛丽 meet for the first time and are finding out each other's nationalities and those of their families and friends.

xiǎo míng　nǐ hǎo
小明：你好！
mǎ lì　nǐ hǎo
玛丽：你好！
xiǎo míng　wǒ shì zhōng guó rén　nǐ shì yīng guó rén ma
小明：我是中国人。你是英国人吗？
mǎ lì　wǒ shì yīng guó rén
玛丽：我是英国人。
xiǎo míng　nǐ bà ba shì yīng guó rén ma
小明：你爸爸是英国人吗？
mǎ lì　wǒ bà ba shì yīng guó rén　nǐ mā ma shì zhōng guó rén ma
玛丽：我爸爸是英国人。你妈妈是中国人吗？
xiǎo míng　shì de　nà shì nǐ péng you ma
小明：是的。那是你朋友吗？
mǎ lì　nà shì wǒ péng you
玛丽：那是我朋友。
xiǎo míng　tā shì mǎ lái xī yà rén ma
小明：他是马来西亚人吗？
mǎ lì　shì de　tā shì mǎ lái xī yà rén
玛丽：是的，他是马来西亚人。

Dialogue B

小明 and 玛丽 are sharing their family photo albums with each other.

mǎ lì　tā shì nǐ gē ge ma
玛丽：他是你哥哥吗？
xiǎo míng　tā shì wǒ péng you　tā shì nǐ jiě jie ma
小明：他是我朋友。她是你姐姐吗？
mǎ lì　tā shì wǒ jiě jie　zhè shì nǐ mèi mei ma
玛丽：她是我姐姐。这是你妹妹吗？
xiǎo míng　zhè shì wǒ péng you　zhè shì nǐ dì di ma
小明：这是我朋友。这是你弟弟吗？
mǎ lì　shì de　zhè shì wǒ dì di　zhè shì nǐ bà ba ma
玛丽：是的，这是我弟弟。这是你爸爸吗？
xiǎo míng　zhè shì wǒ bà ba　nà shì nǐ péng you ma
小明：这是我爸爸。那是你朋友吗？
mǎ lì　shì　nà shì wǒ péng you
玛丽：是，那是我朋友。
xiǎo míng　zhè shì nǐ mā ma ma
小明：这是你妈妈吗？
mǎ lì　zhè shì wǒ mā ma　tā shì nǐ mā ma ma
玛丽：这是我妈妈。她是你妈妈吗？
xiǎo míng　shì de
小明：是的。

Vocabulary

wǒ	我	I; me
nǐ nín	你/您	you; (respectful) you
tā	他	he; him
tā	她	she; her
zhè	这	this
nà	那	that
péng you	朋友	friend(s)
jiā	家	home; family
jiě jie	姐姐	elder sister
dì di	弟弟	younger brother
gē ge	哥哥	elder brother
mèi mei	妹妹	younger sister
mā ma	妈妈	mother
bà ba	爸爸	father
yé ye	爷爷	paternal grandpa
nǎi nai	奶奶	paternal grandma
rén	人	people; person
yīng guó rén	英国人	British
zhōng guó rén	中国人	Chinese
mǎ lái xī yà	马来西亚	Malaysia
wài guó	外国	foreign country
wài guó rén	外国人	foreigner
xiǎo míng	小明	Xiaoming (name)
mǎ lì	玛丽	Mary (name)
hàn nà	汉娜	Hannah (name)
shì	是	to be
shì de	是（的）	yes
ma	吗	(particle)

Grammar

1 是 (shì, to be)

In a simple statement, 是 is used to identify or define the subject, and is followed by a noun/noun phrase. It can be translated as the English verb 'to be' in its many forms such as 'are', 'is', 'am', 'was', 'were'.

- 他是中国人。He is Chinese. ('Chinese' is a noun and identity.)
- 她是我姐姐。She is my elder sister. ('my elder sister' is a noun phrase and identity.)

2 吗 (ma, particle)

吗 is one of the most useful Chinese particles. It has no meaning on its own but turns a statement into a yes/no question, as in 'Do you … ?', 'Is she … ?', 'Will they … ?', etc. It is attached to the end of a statement and followed by a question mark.

他是英国人吗？(a yes/no question)

他是英国人。(a statement/an answer)

Tip

The word order in the question is the same as in the statement, so the only difference between them is whether or not you put 吗 at the end of the sentence. It is a question if you do and it is a statement or an answer if you don't.

Practice text 1

你好！我是小明，我是中国人。
我的爸爸、妈妈、姐姐、弟弟是中国人。
汉娜是我朋友，她是马来西亚人。
她的爸爸、爷爷、奶奶是马来西亚人，她妈妈是中国人。

1 请阅读课文，选择正确答案。Based on the Practice text, identify the correct statements below.

A 小明是中国人。
B 小明的妈妈是英国人。
C 汉娜是小明的朋友。
D 汉娜的奶奶是马来西亚人。
E 汉娜的爸爸是中国人。

2 请听录音，给下列图片排序。Number, in your exercise book, the following pictures in the order you hear them on the recording.

3 请用中文写出五位家庭成员。Write the names of five family members in Chinese.

4 请把下列句子翻译成中文。Translate the following sentences into Chinese.

A I am Mary. She is my elder sister. He is my younger brother.
B I am British. He is my friend. He is a foreigner.
C Xiaoming is my friend. Xiaoming is Chinese.

第二章 家人和宠物

Dialogue A

亚当 and 汉娜 are exchanging information about their family members.

yà dāng　zhè shì wǒ yé ye
亚当：这是我爷爷。

hàn nà　tā hěn shuài　tā máng ma
汉娜：他很帅。他忙吗？

yà dāng　bù　tā bù máng　tā hěn gāo xìng
亚当：不，他不忙，他很高兴。

hàn nà　nǐ bà ba　mā ma hěn máng ma
汉娜：你爸爸、妈妈很忙吗？

yà dāng　tā men hěn máng
亚当：他们很忙。

hàn nà　wǒ jiě jie hǎo kàn ma
汉娜：我姐姐好看吗？

yà dāng　nǐ jiě jie hěn hǎo kàn　nǐ bà ba gāo ma
亚当：你姐姐很好看。你爸爸高吗？

hàn nà　tā hěn gāo　wǒ mā ma bù gāo
汉娜：他很高。我妈妈不高。

yà dāng　nǐ nǎi nai shì yìn ní rén ma
亚当：你奶奶是印尼人吗？

hàn nà　tā shì yìn ní rén　tā hěn hǎo kàn
汉娜：她是印尼人，她很好看。

Dialogue B

亚当 and 汉娜 are talking about their pets.

hàn nà　zhè shì wǒ de tù zi　tā kě ài ma
汉娜：这是我的兔子。她可爱吗？

yà dāng　tā hěn kě ài　tā dà ma
亚当：她很可爱。她大吗？

hàn nà　bù　tā hěn xiǎo
汉娜：不，她很小。

yà dāng　māo shì nǐ nǎi nai de ma
亚当：猫是你奶奶的吗？

hàn nà　shì　tā de māo hěn hǎo kàn
汉娜：是，她的猫很好看。

yà dāng　nà shì nǐ de jīn yú ma
亚当：那是你的金鱼吗？

hàn nà　nà shì wǒ de jīn yú　tā hěn xiǎo
汉娜：那是我的金鱼，他很小。

yà dāng　mǎ shì nǐ bà ba de ma
亚当：马是你爸爸的吗？

hàn nà　bú shì　mǎ shì wǒ jiě jie de
汉娜：不是，马是我姐姐的。

yà dāng　tā de mǎ hěn dà
亚当：她的马很大。

Vocabulary

gāo 高	tall	gǒu 狗	dog	wǒ de 我的	my; mine
gāo xìng 高兴	happy	māo 猫	cat	de 的	(possessive particle)
hǎo 好	good	mǎ 马	horse; pony	yìn ní rén 印尼人	Indonesian
hǎo kàn 好看	pretty	jīn yú 金鱼	goldfish	yà dāng 亚当	Adam (name)
yǒu hǎo 友好	friendly	tù zi 兔子	rabbit	běi jīng 北京	Beijing; Peking
máng 忙	busy	lǎo hǔ 老虎	tiger	shàng hǎi 上海	Shanghai
dà 大	big; large	xióng māo 熊猫	giant panda	xiāng gǎng 香港	Hong Kong
xiǎo 小	small; little	wǒ men 我们	we; us	shū 书	book
shuài 帅	handsome	men 们	(plural for people)	huà 画	painting
kě ài 可爱	cute	hěn 很	very	mén 门	door
chǒng wù 宠物	pet	bù 不	no; not	hái zi 孩子	child; children
dòng wù 动物	animal	nǐ de 你的	your(s)		

Grammar

1 是 (shì, to be)
是 is not used when an adjective follows the subject to form a descriptive sentence.

- 狗很大。The dog is very big. ('big' is an adjective, describing 'the dog'.)
- 小猫很可爱。The little cat is very cute. ('cute' is an adjective, describing 'the little cat'.)

2 的 (de, possessive particle)
的 is a particle indicating the 'possessive' or 'belonging', similar to '…'s/… of …' in English.

- 玛丽的猫很友好。Mary's cat is very friendly. (Mary owns the cat.)
- 你的兔子很可爱。Your rabbit is very lovely. (You own the rabbit.)

Tip
的 can be left out for close family members or friends, such as 我爸爸 (my father), 我朋友 (my friend), or countries, such as 英国画 (English painting).

3 不 (bù, not)
不 is a negative word, treated as an adverb, and is normally placed before a verb, another adverb or an adjective. In writing, 不 is only marked with falling tone, but when the character following 不 is pronounced with falling tone (the fourth tone in Pinyin), the pronunciation of 不 has to be changed to rising tone (the second tone in Pinyin).

- 他的宠物不好看。His pet is not good-looking. (不 (bù) is pronounced with falling tone.)
- 我们不是英国人。We are not British. (不 (bú) is pronounced with rising tone.)

Practice text 2

汉娜的朋友是亚当，他是马来西亚人。他爷爷很帅，
他奶奶很友好。亚当的金鱼很小，很好看。
亚当的妈妈不高，他爸爸很高。他妈妈的猫很小，
很可爱。他弟弟的马不大，不很友好。

1 请阅读课文，用英文回答问题。Answer the following questions in English based on the Practice text and write them in your exercise book.

- **i** What does Adam's grandpa look like?
- **ii** What pet does Adam have?
- **iii** How would you describe the pet?
- **iv** Who in Adam's family is the tall one?
- **v** Who in Adam's family has a cat?
- **vi** How would you describe the cat?
- **vii** What is Adam's little brother's horse like?

2 根据课文，从右栏找出对左栏主语的正确描述。Match the descriptions on the right correctly to the list on the left, according to the Practice text.

i	亚当是	**A**	高
ii	亚当奶奶	**B**	帅
iii	金鱼	**C**	不友好
iv	亚当爸爸	**D**	好看
v	猫	**E**	友好
vi	亚当爷爷	**F**	可爱
vii	马	**G**	不高
viii	亚当妈妈	**H**	汉娜的朋友

3 请听录音，给下列图片排序。Number, in your exercise book, the following pictures in the order you hear them on the recording.

4 请听录音，完成句子。Listen, and write in your exercise book Chinese characters or Pinyin to finish the sentences below.

i 奶奶是__________________人。

ii 那是__________________。

iii 猫__________________。

iv __________________很高。

v 中国人很__________________。

vi 孩子们__________________，很__________________。

5 请将下列句子变成疑问句，然后用否定句回答。Change the following statements into yes/no questions before answering with negative sentences, and write all the sentences down in your exercise book.

Example: 这是我的猫。
—这是你的猫吗？
—这不是我的猫。

i 妈妈的金鱼好看。

ii 爸爸很忙。

iii 爷爷高兴。

iv 我们的马高大。

vi 他们的兔子小。

6 请用中文写80–100个字：Write a paragraph of 80–100 Chinese characters, including information on the following points:

- your nationality
- your family members
- what they look like
- your pets
- your friend.

第三章 爱好

Dialogue A

小明 asks 玛丽 about her hobbies.

xiǎo míng　nǐ de ài hào shì shén me
小明：你的爱好是什么？

mǎ lì　wǒ de ài hào shì kàn diàn yǐng
玛丽：我的爱好是看电影。

xiǎo míng　nǐ xǐ huan měi guó diàn yǐng ma
小明：你喜欢美国电影吗？

mǎ lì　bù xǐ huan　wǒ xǐ huan fǎ guó diàn yǐng
玛丽：不喜欢，我喜欢法国电影。

xiǎo míng　nǐ xǐ huan tī zú qiú ma
小明：你喜欢踢足球吗？

mǎ lì　bù xǐ huan　wǒ bú ài zuò yùn dòng
玛丽：不喜欢，我不爱做运动。

xiǎo míng　nǐ yīng gāi zuò yùn dòng　nǐ xǐ huan tīng yīn yuè ma
小明：你应该做运动。你喜欢听音乐吗？

mǎ lì　wǒ xǐ huan tīng yīn yuè
玛丽：我喜欢听音乐。

xiǎo míng　nǐ cháng cháng tīng shén me yīn yuè
小明：你常常听什么音乐？

mǎ lì　wǒ cháng cháng tīng zhōng guó yīn yuè
玛丽：我常常听中国音乐。

Dialogue B

玛丽 asks 小明 about his hobbies.

mǎ lì　nǐ huì pīng pāng qiú ma
玛丽：你会乒乓球吗？

xiǎo míng　wǒ bú huì　wǒ huì dǎ wǎng qiú
小明：我不会。我会打网球。

mǎ lì　nǐ yě huì dǎ lán qiú ma
玛丽：你也会打篮球吗？

xiǎo míng　huì　wǒ péng you yě dǎ lán qiú
小明：会，我朋友也打篮球。

mǎ lì　nǐ men tiān tiān zuò yùn dòng ma
玛丽：你们天天做运动吗？

xiǎo míng　wǒ men bù néng tiān tiān zuò yùn dòng　wǒ men hěn máng
小明：我们不能天天做运动，我们很忙。

mǎ lì　nǐ kě yǐ tiān tiān kàn diàn shì ma
玛丽：你可以天天看电视吗？

xiǎo míng　wǒ bù néng tiān tiān kàn diàn shì　wǒ wèn mā ma　mā ma shuō bù kě yǐ
小明：我不能天天看电视。我问妈妈，妈妈说不可以。

mǎ lì　nǐ mā ma bú ài kàn diàn shì ma
玛丽：你妈妈不爱看电视吗？

xiǎo míng　tā hěn ài kàn diàn shì　tā tiān tiān kàn diàn shì
小明：她很爱看电视。她天天看电视。

Vocabulary

xǐ huan	喜欢	to like
ài	爱	to love
xiǎng	想	to think; to want
yào	要	to want; to need; to request
huì	会	to know; to be able to; meeting
néng	能	can; be able to
kě yǐ	可以	may; allowed
yīng gāi	应该	should; ought to
yě	也	also
dōu	都	both; all
cháng cháng	常（常）	often
tīng	听	to listen
shuō shuō huà	说/说话	to say; to talk
kàn	看	to read; to see; to watch
dǎ	打	to strike; to play
tī	踢	to kick; to play
jiāo	教	to teach
zuò	做	to do; to become
wèn	问	to ask
qù	去	to go
ài hào	爱好	hobby
kāi xīn	开心	happy
huà huà er	画画儿	to draw; to paint
lán qiú	篮球	basketball
zú qiú	足球	football
wǎng qiú	网球	tennis
pīng pāng qiú	乒乓球	table tennis
yǔ máo qiú	羽毛球	badminton
yóu yǒng	游泳	to swim; swimming
yùn dòng	运动	sport
yīn yuè	音乐	music
diàn yǐng	电影	film
diàn shì	电视	TV
diàn yǐng yuàn	电影院	cinema
shāng diàn	商店	shop
shén me	什么	what
tiān tiān měi tiān	天天/每天	every day
lǎo shī	老师	teacher
míng xīng	明星	famous person; star
míng rén	名人	celebrity
wèi shén me	为什么	why
nǎr nǎ lǐ	哪儿/哪里	where

Grammar

1 Verbs 看 (kàn), 打 (dǎ) and 踢 (tī)

- 看 is used for actions that are carried out by the eyes, for example 'to read', 'to visit/see', 'to look', or 'to observe'.
- 打 is a verb for striking actions by hands or tools held in your hands like 'to hit', 'to strike', or 'to beat', and in sporting events, it is usually translated as 'to play'.
- 踢 means 'to kick' (with your foot), so it is used for playing football and translated as 'to play'.

2 There are some special verbs in Chinese that accompany a main verb to give more emphasis or aspect to a sentence. The most commonly used are 喜欢 (to like), 爱 (to love), 想 (to want/think of), 要 (to want/need) and 会 (can/to know). These can also function as the main verb to go before the object of a sentence.

- 我喜欢打网球。I like playing tennis. ('like' accompanies the main verb 'playing'.)
- 我喜欢网球。I like tennis. ('like' is the main verb.)
- 我想看妈妈。I want to visit my mother. ('want to' accompanies the main verb 'visit'.)
- 我想妈妈。I am missing my mother. ('missing' is the main verb.)
- 我弟弟要踢足球。My younger brother wants to play football. ('wants to' accompanies the main verb 'play'.)
- 我弟弟要足球。My younger brother wants a football. ('wants' is the main verb, meaning 'wants to get'.)

3 These verbs can also be accompanied by certain adverbs like 很 (very/very much), 也 (also), 都 (both/all), 常 (常) (often), etc.

- 她很喜欢打网球。She likes playing tennis very much.
- 爸爸常常想看足球。My father often wants to watch football.
- 我们都爱英国电影。We all love British films.

4 Some verbs in Chinese function as 'modal verbs' in English, for example, 能 (can/to be able to), 可以 (may/allowed to) and 应该 (should/ought to), and they are placed before the main verb of a sentence.

- 我能教你画画。I can teach you how to draw.
- 妈妈，我可以看电视吗？Mum, may I watch TV?
- 你应该多做运动。You should exercise more.

5 什么 (shén me, what)

When 什么 is used as a question word for an interrogative sentence, it does not necessarily go at the beginning. Its place in a question normally reflects that of the answer in a statement, with no change in the word order for other parts of the sentence.

- 你的爱好是什么？What is your hobby?
  我的爱好是音乐。My hobby is music.
- 他们喜欢看什么？What do they like to watch?
  他们喜欢看电影。They like to watch films.

Tip

	As a main verb	Accompanying a main verb	Accompanied by an adverb
喜欢	我喜欢网球。	我喜欢打网球。	我非常喜欢打网球。
爱	姐姐不爱音乐。	姐姐不爱听音乐。	姐姐也不爱听音乐。
想	你想妈妈吗？	你想看妈妈吗？	你很想看妈妈吗？
要	弟弟要足球。	弟弟要踢足球。	
会	我不会篮球。	我不会打篮球。	
能		妹妹能打乒乓球。	
可以		哥哥可以天天做运动吗？	
应该		你应该天天做运动。	

Practice text 3

我是林明。我的家人都爱做运动。爸爸会打网球，也会踢足球。姐姐喜欢画画、听音乐、看电影。她常常去电影院看英国电影。打球是我的爱好：篮球、网球、羽毛球，我都喜欢。我弟弟很小，不能打球。他喜欢小动物，他的小猫很可爱。妈妈喜欢游泳，也教姐姐游泳。她们很忙，不能天天游泳。我的运动老师说，我们应该常常运动，天天开心。

1 请阅读课文，回答问题。Read the Practice text, and write your answers in your exercise book in Chinese.

- i 林明的家人爱做什么？
- ii 他姐姐常常看什么电影？
- iii 林明喜欢做什么运动？
- iv 他弟弟的宠物是什么？
- v 他妈妈的爱好是什么？
- vi 他的运动老师说什么？

2 同学们在谈论他们的爱好。请听录音，选择正确的图片。The students are talking about their hobbies. Listen to the recording and choose the correct picture. Write your answers in your exercise book.

i 小刚　ii 小丽　iii 小海　iv 小英　v 小木

3 请听对一名中学生的采访，并用中文或拼音回答问题。Listen to an interview with a middle school student, and answer the questions. You may write your answers in Chinese characters or Pinyin.

i 王英的爱好是什么？

ii 谁是她的老师？

[PAUSE]

iii 她哥哥的爱好是什么？

iv 他想做什么？

4 请用中文写出你在运动场上看到什么。Write in Chinese five things you see in a sportsground.

5 请用中文写80–100个字，说说你的家人和爱好。Write a passage of 80–100 Chinese characters on your family and hobbies. You may include the following points:

- 你的家人；
- 你们喜欢做什么；
- 你们常常去哪儿；
- 你喜欢天天做什么。

第四章 周末

Dialogue A

It is your first day at a new school and your teacher is getting to know you.

lǎo shī　nǐ jiā zài nǎr
老师：你家在哪儿？

nǐ　wǒ jiā zài shàng hǎi
你：我家在上海。

lǎo shī　nǐ jiā yǒu shén me rén
老师：你家有什么人？

nǐ　wǒ jiā yǒu yé ye nǎi nai bà ba mā ma gē ge hé wǒ
你：我家有爷爷、奶奶、爸爸、妈妈、哥哥和我。

lǎo shī　nǐ jiā lǐ yǒu chǒng wù ma
老师：你家里有宠物吗？

nǐ　yǒu wǒ men yǒu piào liang de māo
你：有，我们有漂亮的猫。

lǎo shī　nǐ yǒu bǐ yǒu ma
老师：你有笔友吗？

nǐ　wǒ méi yǒu bǐ yǒu
你：我没有笔友。

lǎo shī　nǐ zhōu mò xǐ huan zuò shén me
老师：你周末喜欢做什么？

nǐ　wǒ xǐ huan gēn jiā rén yì qǐ qù gōng yuán
你：我喜欢跟家人一起去公园。

Dialogue B

Frank (弗兰克) is in China and has persuaded a stranger on the bus to practise Chinese with him.

fú lán kè　xiǎo jiě nǐ xìng shén me
弗兰克：小姐，你姓什么？

mǎ xiǎo yīng　wǒ xìng mǎ
马小英：我姓马。

fú lán kè　nǐ jiào shén me míng zi
弗兰克：你叫什么名字？

mǎ xiǎo yīng　wǒ jiào mǎ xiǎo yīng
马小英：我叫马小英。

fú lán kè　nǐ qù nǎr
弗兰克：你去哪儿？

mǎ xiǎo yīng　wǒ qù yú lè zhōng xīn de wán jù diàn
马小英：我去娱乐中心的玩具店。

fú lán kè　nǐ qù mǎi dōng xi ma
弗兰克：你去买东西吗？

mǎ xiǎo yīng　bù wǒ shì shāng diàn jīng lǐ
马小英：不，我是商店经理。

fú lán kè　wán jù diàn yǒu chǒng wù de wán jù ma
弗兰克：玩具店有宠物的玩具吗？

mǎ xiǎo yīng　méi yǒu wǒ men zhǐ yǒu xiǎo hái zi men de wán jù
马小英：没有，我们只有小孩子们的玩具。

Vocabulary

yǒu	有	to have; there be
méi yǒu	没有	not have
zài	在	to be (located)
rèn shi	认识	to know; understanding
xué xué xí	学/学习	to learn; to study
lái	来	to come
chī chī fàn	吃/吃饭	to eat
hē	喝	to drink
dàn gāo	蛋糕	cake
chá	茶	tea
kā fēi	咖啡	coffee
qiǎo kè lì	巧克力	chocolate
shuǐ	水	water
xiān sheng	先生	Mr
tài tai	太太	Mrs
ài ren	爱人	partner; spouse
xiǎo jiě	小姐	Miss
shāng rén	商人	businessman
jīng lǐ	经理	manager
yī shēng	医生	doctor
gōng zuò	工作	to work; job
huà jiā	画家	artist
hù shi	护士	nurse
jì zhě	记者	journalist
zuò jiā	作家	author
lín jū	邻居	neighbour
yú lè zhōng xīn	娱乐中心	leisure centre
dòng wù yuán	动物园	zoo
fàn diàn fàn guǎn	饭店/饭馆	restaurant
jù chǎng	剧场	theatre
měi shù guǎn	美术馆	art gallery
kā fēi guǎn	咖啡馆	café
gōng yuán	公园	park
zhǐ	只	only
gēn hé	跟/和	with; and
yì qǐ yí kuàir	一起/一块儿	together
xìng	姓	(to be) surname(d)
jiào	叫	to call/to be called
míng míng zi	名/名字	name
bǐ yǒu	笔友	penfriend
yùn dòng yuán	运动员	athlete
mǎi	买	to buy
duō	多	a lot; much; many
shǎo	少	few/less
dōng xi	东西	things
wán jù	玩具	toy
dàn shì kě shì	但是/可是	but
piào liang	漂亮	beautiful
fēi cháng	非常	extremely
zhī dào	知道	to know
fú zhuāng diàn	服装店	clothes shop
zhōu mò	周末	weekend
xīng qī	星期	week
xīng qī yī	星期一	Monday
xīng qī èr	星期二	Tuesday
xīng qī sān	星期三	Wednesday
xīng qī sì	星期四	Thursday
xīng qī wǔ	星期五	Friday
xīng qī liù	星期六	Saturday
xīng qī tiān rì	星期天/日	Sunday
huáng lǐ lín liú mǎ wáng wú zhāng zhào	黄 李 林 刘 马 王 吴 张 赵	(common Chinese surnames)

Grammar

1 Chinese numerals

1–10	11–20	21–30	100–1,000,000
yī yāo 一/幺	shí yī 十一	èr shí yī 二十一	yì bǎi 一百
èr liǎng 二/两	shí èr 十二	èr shí èr 二十二	yì qiān 一千
sān 三	shí sān 十三	èr shí sān 二十三	yí wàn 一万
sì 四	shí sì 十四	èr shí sì 二十四	shí wàn 十万
wǔ 五	shí wǔ 十五	èr shí wǔ 二十五	yì bǎi wàn 一百万
liù 六	shí liù 十六	èr shí liù 二十六	
qī 七	shí qī 十七	èr shí qī 二十七	
bā 八	shí bā 十八	èr shí bā 二十八	
jiǔ 九	shí jiǔ 十九	èr shí jiǔ 二十九	
shí 十	èr shí 二十	sān shí 三十	

Tips

- The number 'one' has two expressions, with 幺 used mostly in spoken Chinese, and the number 'two' also has two expressions, which will be explained in Chapter 8.
- Chinese has a unit word for 'ten thousand' but not for 'million', while English is the opposite.

2 有 (yǒu, to have/there be)
For the English structure 'there is/are …', Chinese has no equivalent phrase, but uses 有 to express 'existence'. Therefore, for sentences such as 'There are British people in China', we need to turn the structure into 'somewhere has something'. The sentence will simply become 'China has British people.'

Tip

有 has its own negative word, 没, to form the phrase 没有, while all the other verbs use 不 for negation.

- 中国有英国人。There are British people in China.
- 娱乐中心有咖啡馆。There is a café in the leisure centre.
- 有一个人是记者。There is a person who is a journalist. (This sentence does not require a 'place', so the word order is roughly the same in both English and Chinese.)

3 在 (zài, to be located in, at, on or to be somewhere)
在 is a verb which can be used on its own or accompanied by a preposition word such as in, on or at (which will be discussed in Chapter 6).

- 剧场在公园。The theatre is in the park.
- 妈妈在饭店吗？Is my mother in the restaurant?
- 爸爸不在家，他在美术馆。My father is not at home. He is in the art gallery.

4 姓 (xìng, surname) and 名 (míng, given name)

A Most Chinese surnames consist of single characters which are predominantly fathers' family names. Given names consist of one or two characters. In Chinese, surnames come before given names and titles are also preceded by surnames.

	In Chinese with surname first	In English with surname last	Sounds like
With job title	王老师	Teacher Wang	Wang teacher
Ordinary title	张先生	Mr Zhang	Zhang Mr
Full name	马文丽	Wenli Ma	Ma Wenli

B 小 and 大 are widely used in given names and parents often choose characters that express their aspirations and wishes for their newborn children.

Chinese given names	English translation	Implied meanings
小明	Xiaoming	Brightness/intelligence
小花	Xiaohua	Pleasantness (like a flower)
大力	Dali	Strength
大山	Dashan	Steadfastness (like a mountain)

Tip

When addressing young people and senior, use 小 and 老 respectively, such as 小王 and 老王.

C When translating foreign names, the sound 'r' is often converted into the sound 'l', such as:

Mary: 玛丽 (mǎ lì) Frank: 弗兰克 (fú lán kè) Brown: 布朗 (bù lǎng) Gregory: 格里高利 (gé lǐ gāo lì)

5 家 (jiā)

家 is a very useful character, with 'home' being its original meaning. It can also be attached to other characters or words indicating an area of study or a subject to form a name for a job or profession.

画 (to draw) → 画家 (artist) 作 (job) → 作家 (author) 科学 (science) → 科学家 (scientist)

6 和 (hé), 跟 (gēn) and 也 (yě)

Unlike the English word 'and', which can be used to link verb phrases and sentences, the Chinese 和 and 跟 can only link nouns, noun phrases and pronouns. 也 is a better choice for verb phrases.

- 她喜欢喝茶、吃巧克力。She likes to drink tea and eat chocolate.
- 我哥哥爱看小说，我也爱看小说。My brother loves reading novels and I also love reading novels.
- 他和朋友们喜欢踢足球，也喜欢打篮球。He and his friends like to play football and play basketball.

Practice text 4

小李：

你好！

我周末非常高兴。你知道吗？星期六和星期天我跟哥哥去爸爸的朋友黄先生家。我们很高兴认识黄先生的爱人黄太太。黄太太的工作是教画画。我哥哥也想学画画，想做画家。黄太太说他应该常常去美术馆看名人的画，能学到很多。黄先生不会画画，他是商人。

星期六我们一起去咖啡馆喝咖啡，他们的邻居李小姐也想来，但是她的工作是医生，天天都很忙，不能来。在咖啡馆，黄太太只喝水。我很想喝中国茶，可是咖啡馆没有茶。

星期天我们去中国饭店吃了很多中国蛋糕，也吃了不少法国巧克力。

你的周末好吗？

你的朋友
林刚

1 请阅读课文，选择正确的答案。Read the Practice text, and choose the best answer to each question.

i 为什么林刚很高兴？

A 林刚周末去朋友家。

B 林刚去黄先生家。

C 林刚去奶奶家。

ii 黄太太说林刚哥哥应该去哪儿学画画？

A 美术馆

B 黄太太家

C 美术学院

iii 黄先生做什么工作？

A 老师

B 商人

C 画家

iv 他们在哪儿吃了很多东西？

A 咖啡馆

B 动物园

C 饭店

2 朋友们在谈论他们想要做的工作。请听录音，选择正确的图片。Some friends are talking about the jobs they want to do. Listen to the recording and write down the correct answer according to the pictures.

i 王文　　ii 李兰　　iii 林力　　iv 马英　　v 小林

3 请用下面的词语造句。Write out five sentences in Chinese in your exercise book using the words given in the box.

Verb	Possible objects	Examples
吃	鸡、鱼、菜、巧克力、蛋糕	姐姐喜欢吃蛋糕，她在咖啡店工作。
喝	茶、咖啡、水	
打	网球、篮球、乒乓球	周末我喜欢跟朋友小明在公园打网球。
踢	足球、球	
叫	小明、小英、美美	

4 请用中文写80–100个字，说说你的朋友。内容如下：Write a passage of 80–100 Chinese characters about your friend. You may include the following:

- 你的朋友叫什么名字；
- 他的家人做什么工作；
- 你朋友喜欢什么运动；
- 你周末跟他/她一起做些什么；
- 你为什么很喜欢他/她。

第五章 暑假

Dialogue A

你从中国回来了，在和朋友说话。You have returned from China and are talking to your British friend.

péng you　jīn nián hán jià nǐ qù le nǎ lǐ
朋友：今年寒假你去了哪里？

nǐ　wǒ gēn tóng xué qù le běi jīng
你：我跟同学去了北京。

péng you　wèi shén me qù běi jīng
朋友：为什么去北京？

nǐ　wǒ men qù xué huà zhōng guó huà
你：我们去学画中国画。

péng you　nǐ men mǎi le shén me jì niàn pǐn
朋友：你们买了什么纪念品？

nǐ　wǒ men mǎi le yì shù pǐn
你：我们买了艺术品。

péng you　běi jīng de fēng jǐng hǎo ma
朋友：北京的风景好吗？

nǐ　běi jīng de fēng jǐng zhēn piào liang
你：北京的风景真漂亮。

péng you　nǐ men zuò le shén me huó dòng
朋友：你们做了什么活动？

nǐ　wǒ men qù pá shān le
你：我们去爬山了。

Dialogue B

你在中国参加夏令营，在跟一个美国同学说话。You are in a summer camp in China, talking to a student from the USA.

tóng xué　zuó tiān nǐ qù xī hú le ma
同学：昨天你去西湖了吗？

nǐ　qù le　wǒ hěn xǐ huan xī hú
你：去了，我很喜欢西湖。

tóng xué　nǐ men guó jiā yě yǒu piào liang de fēng jǐng ma
同学：你们国家也有漂亮的风景吗？

nǐ　yǒu　yīng guó de fēng jǐng yě fēi cháng měi lì
你：有，英国的风景也非常美丽。

tóng xué　yīng guó de dōng xi dōu hěn guì ma
同学：英国的东西都很贵吗？

nǐ　qù nián hěn guì　jīn nián dōng xi dōu pián yi le
你：去年很贵，今年东西都便宜了。

tóng xué　jīn tiān nǐ xiǎng qù nǎr
同学：今天你想去哪儿？

nǐ　wǒ xiǎng qù shū diàn
你：我想去书店。

tóng xué　nǐ yào mǎi shén me
同学：你要买什么？

nǐ　wǒ yào mǎi zá zhì
你：我要买杂志。

Vocabulary

le	了	(particle for tense)
qù nián	去年	last year
jīn nián	今年	this year
zuó tiān	昨天	yesterday
jīn tiān	今天	today
shǔ jià qī	暑假/期	summer holiday
hán jià	寒假	winter holiday
wǎng bā	网吧	internet café
diàn nǎo	电脑	computer
shū diàn	书店	bookstore
yóu yǒng chí	游泳池	swimming pool
tú shū guǎn	图书馆	library
shí zhuāng diàn	时装店	boutiques
zá zhì	杂志	magazine
shū fǎ	书法	calligraphy
xiǎo rén shū	小人书	picture book
gōng yì pǐn	工艺品	handicraft
zhēn	真	real; really
bó wù guǎn	博物馆	museum
shì zhōng xīn	(市)中心	(city) centre
yīn wéi	因为	because
suǒ yǐ	所以	so; therefore
jì niàn pǐn	纪念品	souvenir
shǒu biǎo	手表	wristwatch
guì	贵	expensive
pián yi	便宜	cheap
mài	卖	to sell
xiān	先	first
rán hòu	然后	then
cóng	从	from
xiě xìn	写(信)	to write (a letter)
xià lìng yíng	夏令营	summer camp
huí huí lái	回/回来	to return
pá shān	爬山	to climb a mountain
guó guó jiā	国/国家	country
háng zhōu	杭州	(name of a city)
xī hú	西湖	(name of a lake)
fēng jǐng	风景	scenery
měi lì	美丽	beautiful
lǐ wù	礼物	present; gift
tóng xué	同学	classmate
xué shēng	学生	student
gěi sòng gěi	给/送给	to give to/for
hǎo wánr	好玩儿	fun

Grammar

1 In statements, Chinese verbs mostly function the same way as verbs in other languages.

- 林先生是中国人。Mr Lin is Chinese.
- 刘小姐有照相机。Miss Liu has a camera.
- 他们不认识。They do not know each other.
- 弗兰克喜欢游泳。Frank likes swimming.

However, in many languages, verbs may have different forms, showing tense, gender, number, etc. These forms do not exist in Chinese grammar. The sentence below demonstrates the vagueness about when the action takes place.

- 王太太去博物馆，他们也去博物馆。Mrs Wang goes to the museum and they also go to the museum. (This could be either a past event or a future event.)

2 Chinese verbs do not change their forms for grammatical purposes. Instead, there are words that indicate a specific time when an action takes place.

去年	赵经理去年**在**美国。	'last year' indicates that he **was** in the USA.
明年	张小姐明年**去**法国。	'next year' indicates that she **will go to** France.
暑假	大山暑假**打**篮球。	Whether he **played or is going to play** depends on which summer holiday is closer, the one just gone or the next one.
周末	马林周末**买**纪念品。	Whether he **bought or is going to buy** depends on which weekend is closer, the past one or the forthcoming one.
星期一	刘小明星期一**去**火车站。	He (probably) **is going to** the train station.
明天	王小花明天**吃**法国菜。	'tomorrow' indicates she **will eat** French food.

3 了 (le, particle)

A 了 is used to indicate a finished action by attaching it to the verb of the sentence.

- 他暑假去了法国。He went to France in the summer holiday.
- 我们买了好东西。We bought good things.
- 他们去了电影院。They went to the cinema.

B When 了 goes to the end of a sentence, it emphasises a proven fact or an event which has taken place very recently. Compare the following sentences.

- 赵太太去了美国。Mrs Zhao went to the USA.
- 赵太太去美国了。Mrs Zhao has gone to the USA. (implying 'she is not here now')
- 我妹妹买了菜。My younger sister bought vegetables.
- 我妹妹买菜了。My young sister has bought the vegetables. (emphasizing on the task being done)

C The negative word for 了 is 没 (有) + verb (and without 了).

赵太太没去美国。Mrs Zhao did not go to the USA.

有 + length of time + 没 + action + 了 = have not done something for a certain length of time.

- 我们有两个星期没吃中国饭了！We have not had Chinese meals for two weeks!
- 爸爸有一个星期没回家了。My father has not been back home for a week.

D 了 can also be used to indicate a change of situation, and it should go to the end of a declarative sentence. It can be accompanied by a time reference, and when translating into English, 'now' or 'any more' can be added.

- 我喜欢她了。I like her now. (implying 'I didn't before')
- 今年东西贵了。Things are getting more expensive this year. (implying 'last year they were cheaper')

Practice text 5

去年暑假我跟同学一起去了中国杭州的夏令营。那里也有很多日本学生和美国学生。我们每天都学书法和中国音乐，也学画中国画。夏令营有游泳池、网吧和图书馆。图书馆有很多电脑、小人书和杂志。

星期六我们去了市中心买纪念品。我买了很多礼物送给家人。我先买了漂亮的手表送给姐姐，然后买了中国时装送给妈妈。我们也去了博物馆。那儿的商店卖工艺品，非常漂亮，可是我没买，因为很贵，不便宜。

星期天我们去了西湖。你知道吗？那儿的风景真美丽！

我们有两个星期没跟家人在一起了！可是我们都不想回家！因为夏令营非常好玩儿！

1 请阅读课文，用中文回答问题，并把答案写在练习本上。Based on the Practice text, answer the following questions in Chinese and write them in your exercise book.

- **i** 夏令营在哪儿？
- **ii** 学生们都从什么国家来？
- **iii** 他们每天都学习什么？
- **iv** 图书馆有什么？
- **v** 星期六"我"和同学一起去了哪里？
- **vi** "我"为什么没买工艺品？
- **vii** "我"喜欢西湖的什么？

2 小林参加一个夏令营，正在和那里的老师谈话。请听录音，选出夏令营提供哪些设施。Xiao Lin is at a summer camp, talking to a teacher working there. Listen to the recording, and choose the five facilities shown in the pictures.

A

B

C

D

E

F

G

H

I

3 请用中文写出你在一个夏令营看到什么。Write in Chinese five things you see at a summer camp.

4 扩展练习。Look at the example question and answers below, then write out your own answers to the questions given, using the suggestions provided. This exercise can also be used for speaking practice.

	Questions	**Sample answers**
Example:	你的爱好是什么？ What is your hobby?	• 我的爱好是音乐。 • 我喜欢学音乐。 • 我天天在学校学音乐。 • 我喜欢学音乐，因为很好玩儿。
You do it:	周末你去了什么地方？ Where did you go at the weekend?	• I went to the city centre at the weekend. • I like the city centre because I like shopping. • I like to go to the city centre with my friends. • My brother did not go with us because he had swimming lessons. • I also went to the park at the weekend. • I like going to the park because the scenery is beautiful.
	你昨天买了什么？ What did you buy yesterday?	• I bought a Chinese magazine yesterday. • I also bought an English book. • My hobby is reading books. • I read (books) every day. • My friend Xiaoming bought a Chinese book because he is learning Chinese. • I want to buy a basketball tomorrow because I want to play basketball with my friends in the park.

5 你和同学一起参加了一个夏令营。请给你的奶奶写一封150字左右的信，信里说：You went to a summer camp with your classmates. Write a letter of about 150 Chinese characters to your grandma and say:

- 你们去了什么地方；
- 那里的风景好吗；
- 你买了什么，做了什么；
- 你喜欢那里吗，为什么。

Unit test 1

1 填空练习。Group the family members by their genders and write the answers in your exercise book.

Family members				Female	Male
爷爷	奶奶	弟弟	姐姐		
妈妈	爸爸	哥哥	妹妹		

2 组词。Write in your exercise book as many words as possible containing the following characters.

电	
球	
国	
人	
家	
店	
书	
馆	

3 请阅读下面的短文。Read the passage.

中学生小明

今年上海英材中学的学生小明周末也很忙。他星期六要去学音乐，星期天去学书法，因为妈妈要他学音乐，爸爸要他学书法。爸爸不会书法，但是很喜欢。小明不能常常跟邻居的孩子一起去公园打篮球。

请用下列词组填空。Fill in the blanks with the correct words chosen from the list below and copy them in your exercise book.

音乐	妈妈	邻居的孩子	帮	不可以	天天	可以	不会

A 上海英材中学的学生小明____________都很忙。
B 星期六他要学____________。
C 爸爸喜欢书法，可是____________。
D 小明周末不能跟____________做运动。

Did you know … ?

lǐ guāng qián
李 光 前

yī jiǔ liù qī nián liù yuè xīn jiā pō shī qù le yí wèi jié chū de ài guó rén shì
一九六七年六月，新加坡失去了一位杰出的爱国人士。
tā jiù shì yuǎn jìn zhù míng de shí yè jiā jiào yù jiā hé cí shàn jiā lǐ guāng qián
他就是远近著名的实业家、教育家和慈善家李光前
xiān sheng
先生。

lǐ guāng qián chū shēng yú zhōng guó fú jiàn shěng hěn xiǎo jiù gēn jiā rén yí mín dào
李光前出生于中国福建省，很小就跟家人移民到
xīn jiā pō zài jiē shòu yīng wén jiào yù de tóng shí tā bù hū shì guó yǔ de jiào yù
新加坡。在接受英文教育的同时，他不忽视国语的教育，
jiān chí xué xí céng jīng yí dù huí zhōng guó jìn xiū hàn yǔ
坚持学习。曾经一度回中国进修汉语。

lǐ guāng qián nián qīng shí zài xiàng jiāo yuán chuàng yè shì yè chéng gōng hòu lái
李光前年轻时在橡胶园创业，事业成功。后来
yòu nǔ lì xīng bàn jiào yù bìng juān kuǎn zī zhù guó jiā tú shū guǎn de jiàn shè wèi
又努力兴办教育，并捐款资助国家图书馆的建设，为
xīn jiā pō de wén huà jiào yù zuò chū le jù dà gòng xiàn lǐ guāng qián yì shēng dōu zhù
新加坡的文化教育做出了巨大贡献。李光前一生都助
rén wéi lè cān yù wú shù cí shàn huó dòng zài dōng nán yà gè guó dé dào zī zhù de
人为乐，参与无数慈善活动。在东南亚各国，得到资助的
tú shū guǎn xiǎo xué zhōng xué hé dà xué shǔ bú shèng shǔ
图书馆、小学、中学和大学数不胜数。

2 第二单元 日常活动

Unit 2 Everyday activities

你家房子在哪儿？ Where is your house?

1 How many of these features do you have in your own community? Discuss with a partner.

2 Here are some direction words for you to learn.

fāng xiàng
方 向 direction

dōng biān 东（边）east	xī biān 西（边）west	nán biān 南（边）south	běi biān 北（边）north
dōng nán 东 南 south-east	dōng běi 东 北 north-east	xī nán 西 南 south-west	xī běi 西 北 north-west
dōng fāng 东（方）eastern region		xī fāng 西（方）western region	
nán fāng 南（方）southern region		běi fāng 北（方）northern region	

3 Draw a sketch map of your local area on A4 paper.

Write each Chinese direction word on the map in the correct location.

On separate sticky notes, write the Chinese words for your house, your friend's house and as many other buildings and features that you know.

Stick the notes on your map in the correct locations.

You will refer to your map again in Chapter 8.

第六章 我家房子

Dialogue A

你跟老师说你的新家。You are talking to your teacher about your new home.

lǎo shī　nǐ jiā de fáng zi zěn me yàng
老师：你家的房子怎么样？
nǐ　hěn dà　bù xīn yě bú jiù
你：很大，不新也不旧。
lǎo shī　fáng zi de wài miàn yǒu huā yuán ma
老师：房子的外面有花园吗？
nǐ　yǒu dà huā yuán　lǐ miàn yǒu hěn duō huā cǎo hé shù mù
你：有大花园，里面有很多花草和树木。
lǎo shī　fàn tīng lǐ miàn yǒu shén me jiā jù
老师：饭厅里面有什么家具？
nǐ　yǒu fàn zhuō　yǐ zi hé dēng
你：有饭桌、椅子和灯。
lǎo shī　nǐ de wò shì lǐ yǒu shén me dōng xi
老师：你的卧室里有什么东西？
nǐ　wǒ de wò shì lǐ yǒu cè suǒ　chuáng hé shū jià
你：我的卧室里有厕所、床和书架。
lǎo shī　nǐ jiā zuǒ yòu de lín jū zěn me yàng
老师：你家左右的邻居怎么样？
nǐ　tā men dōu hěn yǒu hǎo
你：他们都很友好。

Dialogue B

你在香港，跟你的新同学说英国的天气。You are in Hong Kong, talking to your new friend about the British weather.

tóng xué　yīng guó tiān qì zěn me yàng
同学：英国天气怎么样？
nǐ　tiān tiān dōu bú tài lěng　yě bú tài rè
你：天天都不太冷，也不太热。
tóng xué　shǔ jià tiān qì zěn me yàng
同学：暑假天气怎么样？
nǐ　cháng cháng xià yǔ　wǒ men bù néng tiān tiān qù wài biān yùn dòng
你：常常下雨，我们不能天天去外边运动。
tóng xué　xià yǔ tiān nǐ zuò shén me
同学：下雨天你做什么？
nǐ　wǒ zhǐ néng zài fáng zi lǐ kàn diàn shì
你：我只能在房子里看电视。
tóng xué　wǒ péng you shuō yīng guó cháng cháng guā fēng　duì ma
同学：我朋友说英国常常刮风，对吗？
nǐ　bú duì　bú guò yīn tiān duō　qíng tiān hěn shǎo
你：不对，不过阴天多，晴天很少。
tóng xué　nǐ xǐ huan shén me tiān qì
同学：你喜欢什么天气？
nǐ　wǒ xǐ huan xià xuě de tiān qì　xuě huā fēi cháng měi lì
你：我喜欢下雪的天气，雪花非常美丽。

Vocabulary

lǐ biān 里边	inside	wò shì 卧室	bedroom	yù bào 预报	forecast
qián biān 前边	in the front/before	wèi shēng jiān 卫生间	bathroom	tài 太	very much; extremely
zuǒ biān 左边	left	fáng jiān wū zi 房间/屋子	room	rè 热	hot
shàng biān 上边	above/on	cè suǒ 厕所	toilet	lěng 冷	cold
zhōng jiān 中间	between/middle	fàn tīng 饭厅	dining room	duì 对	correct
duì miàn 对面	opposite	chú fáng 厨房	kitchen	fēng 风	wind
wài biān 外边	outside	shū fáng 书房	study (room)	guā fēng 刮风	windy
hòu biān 后边	back/after	huā yuán 花园	garden	yǔ 雨	rain
yòu biān 右边	right	huā huā er 花/花儿	flower	xià yǔ 下雨	to rain
xià biān 下边	below/under	shù shù mù 树/树木	tree	yǔ sǎn 雨伞	umbrella
páng biān 旁边	next to/beside	cǎo 草	grass	xuě 雪	snow
zhèr zhè lǐ 这儿/这里	here	zhuō zi 桌子	desk/table	xià xuě 下雪	to snow
nàr nà lǐ 那儿/那里	there	yǐ zi 椅子	chair	wù 雾	fog
gān jìng 干净	clean	shā fā 沙发	sofa	xià wù 下雾	foggy
zhěng qí 整齐	tidy	chuáng 床	bed	yún 云	cloud
shū fu 舒服	well; comfortable	tái dēng dēng 台灯/灯	light; lamp	duō yún 多云	cloudy
xīn 新	new	zěn me yàng 怎(么)样	how is it?	qíng tiān 晴天	clear day
jiù 旧	worn; old	xǐ yī jī 洗衣机	washing machine	yīn tiān 阴天	cloudy day
rè nao 热闹	lively	shū jià 书架	bookshelf	rì cháng 日常	daily
fáng zi 房子	house	jiā jù 家具	furniture	huó dòng 活动	activity
kè tīng 客厅	lounge	tiān qì 天气	weather		

Grammar

1 Talking about weather
There is no equivalent word in Chinese for the English word 'it' when referring to weather. Instead, a specific date or time is needed.

A The simplest way of talking about the weather needs two elements: a subject (noun) + an adjective.

- 昨天冷。It was cold yesterday. (Yesterday cold.)
- 今天不冷。It is not cold today. (Today not cold.)
- 明天热。It is going to be hot tomorrow. (Tomorrow hot.)

B When a subject is followed by a noun, 是 is used.

- 昨天是晴天。Yesterday was a sunny day.
- 今天不是晴天。Today is not a sunny day.
- 明天是阴天。Tomorrow will be a cloudy day.

C There are no adjectives in Chinese to describe the weather such as 'rainy', 'snowy' and 'windy'. Instead, nouns like 'rain', 'snow' and 'wind' are used, accompanied by verbs like 'to fall', 'to have', or 'to blow'.

- 今天**有**小雨。There is going to be light rain today.
- 明天**下**大雪。It will snow heavily tomorrow.
- 星期六**刮**风。It will be windy on Saturday.

Tip
小 and 大 are frequently used to describe the severity of the weather.

D Expressions such as 多云 (a lot of cloud), 多风 (a lot of wind), 多雨 (a lot of rain), 多雪 (a lot of snow) are the closest to 'cloudy', 'windy', 'rainy' and 'snowy'.

- 今天多云。It is very cloudy today. (Today much cloud.)
- 去年多雪。It snowed a lot last year. (Last year much snow.)

E As mentioned in Chapter 5, 了 can indicate a change of situation, so it can be added to the end of a sentence to indicate new or different weather.

- 今天冷了。It has turned cold today.
- 昨天下雨了，也刮大风了。It rained yesterday and was also very gusty.

2 Adjectives

A If the adjective is made up of one character, it is placed before the noun.

旧沙发 old sofa	**热**天 hot day	**大**雨 heavy rain
新椅子 new chairs	**冷**天 cold day	**小**花园 small garden

B If the adjective is made up of two or more characters, 的 is placed between the adjective and the noun.

漂亮**的**家具 beautiful furniture　　舒服**的**卧室 a comfortable bedroom

很小**的**花园 a very small garden　　很大**的**雨 very heavy rain

C 多 and 少 are two adjectives with their own rules. They are normally accompanied by 很 when used to describe nouns and without 的.

很多人 many people　　**很**少人 few people　　**很**多雪 a lot of snow

3 Talking about locations

A Chinese also has preposition phrases, but the word order is the opposite to those in English. The Chinese literal translation for 'on the desk' reads 'the desk on'.

- 书房右边 to the right of the study (study right)
- 桌子下边 under the table (table under)
- 卧室和厕所中间 between the bedroom and the toilet (bedroom and toilet between)

B 在 is a verb, so do not attempt to add 是 (to be) as you would in English. Use 在 to state that something is located somewhere.

The word order is:
Subject (something) + 在 + place (somewhere) + position

饭厅　在　书房　右边。

The dining room is to the right of the study.

C As explained in Chapter 4, a sentence with the structure of 'There are/is something in somewhere' needs to be converted into 'somewhere have/has something'.

The word order is:
somewhere + position + 有 + something

桌子　下边　有　椅子。

There is a chair under the table.

有 can be replaced by 是 with an emphasis on exclusiveness.

- 学校前边有火车站。There is a train station in front of the school.
- 学校前边是火车站。It is the train station in front of the school.

D And, of course, there are simpler sentences than the above examples with the position word used as a place or as the subject of a sentence.

- 洗衣机在里边。The washing machine is inside.
- 厨房在后边。The kitchen is at the back.
- 这儿是我家。Here is my home.
- 学校在那儿。The school is over there.

Practice text 6

小王：

你好！

昨天我去看了我们的新房子，真漂亮！有很多房间。客厅很大，有新灯、新沙发和电视。饭厅在客厅的后边，那里有桌子和椅子。饭厅对面是厨房，洗衣机在厨房里边。爸爸非常喜欢他的书房，他爱看书，可是他的书桌不整齐，因为桌子上有很多书。我的卧室不大，没有很多家具，只有床和书架。床不很新，是我的旧床，但是很舒服，我的玩具在床下边。书架的上边有小灯。爸爸妈妈的卧室有卫生间。

因为新房子在市中心，所以没有花园。妈妈不高兴，因为她很喜欢花草和树木。我们家旁边有咖啡馆、时装店和电影院。电影院在咖啡馆和时装店的中间。这儿天天都很热闹，也很干净。

你周末来看我们的新家，好吗？

你的朋友

小花

1 请阅读课文，然后回答问题。Read the Practice text, and then answer the questions.

- **i** 小花的新房子怎么样？
- **ii** 饭厅在哪儿？
- **iii** 洗衣机在哪儿？
- **iv** 她爸爸的书桌为什么不整齐？
- **v** 小花的房间有什么家具？
- **vi** 小花的妈妈为什么不高兴？
- **vii** 电影院在哪儿？
- **viii** 小花家旁边怎么样？

2 请看图表找出每个城市的天气。Look at the chart and match the weather with each city.

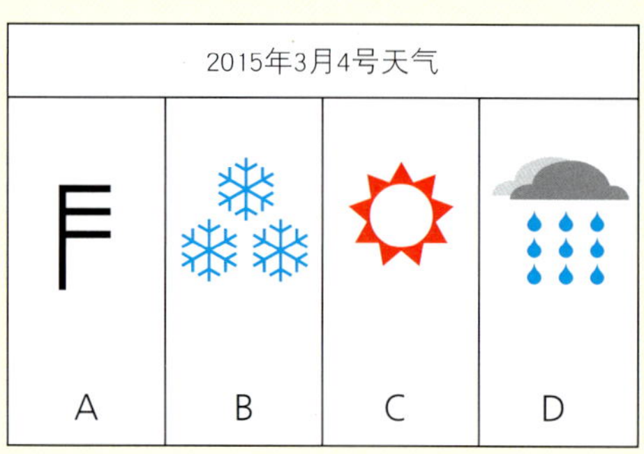

- **i** 北京—大风
- **ii** 上海—晴天
- **iii** 杭州—雨
- **iv** 拉萨—大雪

3 今天是星期天。你在杭州，听下一个星期的天气预报。请看图片。
It's Sunday. You are in Hangzhou, listening to the weather forecast for the next week. Look at the pictures.
请听录音，选择正确的图片回答问题。Listen, and choose the correct answer for each day.

i 星期一 **ii** 星期二 **iii** 星期三 **iv** 星期四 **v** 星期五

4 请用中文写出你在房子里看到什么。Write in Chinese five things you see in a house.

5 记住下面的短语。Treat the following phrases as individual words and learn by heart.

Chinese	English
bǎi huò shāng diàn de dōng biān 百货商店的东边	to the east of the department store
yín háng běi biān 银行北边	to the north of the bank
yóu yǒng chí de qián biān 游泳池的前边	in front of the swimming pool
shū fáng hòu biān 书房后边	behind the study

请将下列句子翻译成中文。Translate the following English sentences into Chinese with the vocabulary given below and write them in your exercise book.

tú shū guǎn 图书馆	xué xiào 学校	chē fáng 车房	huā yuán 花园

i Group A with 在

- The library is to the east of the department store.
- The school is to the north of the bank.
- The garage is in front of the swimming pool.
- The garden is behind the study.

ii Group B with 有

- There is a library to the east of the department store.
- It is a school to the north of the bank.
- There is a garage in front of the swimming pool.
- There is a garden behind the study.

6 你的笔友想知道你住的地方。请给笔友写一封150字左右的信。信里说：
Your penfriend wants to know what the place where you live is like. Write him/her a letter of about 150 Chinese characters and say:

- 你家房子怎么样（房间、花园）；
- 你家旁边有什么好玩儿的地方；
- 你周末去了哪儿，做了什么；
- 你喜欢那儿吗，为什么。

第七章 学校的一天

Dialogue A

明天你去上海，跟老师说。Tomorrow you are going to Shanghai, and you are telling your teacher about it.

shī　nǐ míng tiān jǐ diǎn chū fā
师：你明天几点出发？
nǐ　xià wǔ wǔ diǎn　xià le kè jiù chū fā
你：下午五点，下了课就出发。
shī　nǐ gēn shuí yì qǐ qù
师：你跟谁一起去？
nǐ　wǒ gēn péng you yí kuàir qù
你：我跟朋友一块儿去。
shī　nǐ men zuò shén me qù
师：你们坐什么去？
nǐ　wǒ men zuò huǒ chē qù　huǒ chē liù diǎn líng wǔ fēn cóng chē zhàn chū fā
你：我们坐火车去，火车六点零五分从车站出发。
shī　míng tiān tiān qì zěn me yàng
师：明天天气怎么样？
nǐ　bù lěng bú rè　hěn shū fu
你：不冷不热，很舒服。
shī　nǐ men nǎ tiān huí lai
师：你们哪天回来？
nǐ　xīng qī èr jiù huí lai
你：星期二就回来。

Dialogue B

你在游泳池，跟朋友的姐姐谈话。You are in a swimming pool, talking to a friend's sister.

jiě　nǐ měi tiān jǐ diǎn lái dào yóu yǒng chí
姐：你每天几点来到游泳池？
nǐ　xià wǔ sān diǎn jiù dào le
你：下午三点就到了。
jiě　nǐ zěn me lái yóu yǒng chí
姐：你怎么来游泳池？
nǐ　mā ma kāi chē sòng wǒ lái
你：妈妈开车送我来。
jiě　nǐ nǎ nián xué huì yóu yǒng le
姐：你哪年学会游泳了？
nǐ　wǒ cóng xiǎo jiù huì le
你：我从小就会了。
jiě　nǐ wèi shén me xǐ huan yóu yǒng
姐：你为什么喜欢游泳？
nǐ　yīn wèi wǒ bà ba shì yóu yǒng yùn dòng yuán
你：因为我爸爸是游泳运动员。
jiě　zài xué xiào　shuí jiāo nǐ men yóu yǒng
姐：在学校，谁教你们游泳？
nǐ　wáng lǎo shī jiāo wǒ men　tā yóu yǒng fēi cháng hǎo
你：王老师教我们。他游泳非常好。

Vocabulary

xué xiào	学校	school
jiào shì	教室	classroom
lǐ táng	礼堂	assembly hall
tǐ yù guǎn	体育馆	gym
shàng xué	上学	to go to school
fàng xué xià xué	放学/下学	school finishes
jiāo huàn xué shēng	交换学生	exchange student
kè	课	lesson
shàng kè	上课	lesson starts
xià kè	下课	lesson finishes
bān	班	class
kē mù	科目	subject
lì shǐ	历史	History
hàn yǔ zhōng wén	汉语/中文	Chinese
yīng yǔ yīng wén	英语/英文	English
shù xué	数学	Mathematics
zuò chéng	坐/乘	to go … by; to take
chuán	船	ship; boat
chē chē liàng	车/车辆	vehicle
kāi chē	开车	to drive
sòng	送	to see … off; to deliver

zǒu lù	走路	on foot/walk
qí zì xíng chē	骑自行车	to ride a bicycle
gōng gòng qì chē	公共汽车	bus
huǒ chē	火车	train
fēi jī	飞机	aeroplane
dì tiě	地铁	underground train
qǐ chuáng	起床	to get up
shàng chuáng	上床	to go to bed
shuì shuì jiào	睡/睡觉	to sleep
shàng wǎng	上网	to go online
xiàn zài	现在	now
diǎn diǎn zhōng	点/点钟	o'clock
bàn	半	half
fēn fēn zhōng	分/分钟	minute
kè	刻	quarter
líng	零	zero
jǐ	几	what number; several
shuí/shéi	谁	who
zǎo	早	early
wǎn	晚	late
nǎ	哪	which

zěn me	怎么	how
chū fā	出发	to set off
dào	到	to reach; to get to; to arrive
sàn bù	散步	to walk; to take a stroll
chàng gē	唱歌	to sing a song
jiù	就	already; then; as early as
cái	才	only then; not until
yǐ jīng	已经	already
kāi shǐ	开始	to start
huò huò zhě	或/或者	or
zǎo shang zǎo chén	早上/早晨	morning
zǎo cān zǎo fàn	早餐/早饭	breakfast
shàng wǔ	上午	am
zhōng wǔ	中午	noon
xià wǔ	下午	pm
wǔ cān wǔ fàn	午餐/午饭	lunch
xià wǔ chá	下午茶	afternoon tea
diǎn xīn	点心	snack
wǎn shang	晚上	evening
wǎn cān wǎn fàn	晚餐/晚饭	dinner

Grammar

1 Talking about time

A A verb is not needed for telling the time.

现在几点？What time is it now?

现在三点。It is three o'clock now.

> **Tip**
> When 现在 (now) is used, remember to put it before the time, never after.

B As a general rule, hours comes before minutes.

一点半 one thirty 三点三刻 a quarter to four 五点十分 ten past five

C There is no word in Chinese equivalent to the English 'it' referred to as time. Instead, questions and answers on the time can be very short.

几点？What time is it? 五点。Five o'clock.

D 分 (fēn, minute) is optional for time between 11 to 59. For example, 6:15 can be 六点十五分 and can also be 六点十五, but 6:10 should be 六点十分. For minutes with single digits, 零 must be inserted between the hour and the minute, for example, 23:05 should be 二十三点零五分.

E Morning, noon, afternoon and evening are placed before the time.

上午八点 8 am 中午十二点 12 midday

下午四点 4 pm 晚上十点 10 pm

2 不 (bù) and 没 (méi)

A 不 is used to talk about something that is not true or is not the case.

- 王医生不在图书馆看书。Doctor Wang does not read books in the library.
- 小林不走路上学，他坐地铁。Xiao Lin does not walk to school. He takes the tube.
- 星期三我们不上音乐课。We do not have music lessons on Wednesday.

B 没 is used to indicate that an action did not take place.

- 马太太没和女儿一起买东西。Mrs Ma did not go shopping with her daughter.
- 星期三我们没上音乐课。We did not have music lessons on Wednesday.

3 Adverbials are used to give extra information about time, place, manner, duration, etc.

- 我**下午三点**学画画。I have a painting class at 3 pm. (time)
- 王医生**在图书馆**看书。Doctor Wang read books in the library. (place)
- 马太太**和女儿一起**买东西。Mrs Ma goes shopping with her daughter. (with whom)
- 小林**走路**上学。Xiao Lin walks to school. (transport)
- **星期三**我们上音乐课。We have music lessons on Wednesday. (day)

> **Tip**
> Adverbials are different from subjects, objects and complements.

4 When two or more adverbials appear in one sentence, time normally goes before means of transportation or place.

- 我早上七点在家吃饭。I have breakfast at home at seven in the morning.
- 张校长星期三跟她的先生坐飞机去中国了。Headmaster Zhang flew to China with her husband on Wednesday.

Tip

坐飞机 could be translated as 'fly' or 'by plane', depending on where they are in a sentence.

5 Question words

What day	What time	Who/whom	Which	Where	How
星期几	几点	谁	哪	哪儿/哪里	怎么

In English a question word is usually put at the beginning of the sentence, whereas in Chinese it is usually at the place where the answer would be.

- 刘小姐星期天跟一个朋友坐飞机去了中国。Miss Liu flew to China with a friend on Sunday.
- 刘小姐**星期几**跟一个朋友坐飞机去了中国？What day did Miss Liu fly to China with a friend?
- 刘小姐星期天跟**谁**坐飞机去了中国？Who did Miss Liu fly to China with on Sunday?
- 刘小姐星期天跟一个朋友**怎么**去中国？How did Miss Liu go to China with a friend on Sunday?
- 刘小姐星期天跟一个朋友坐飞机去了**哪儿**？Where did Miss Liu go with a friend by air on Sunday?
- **谁**星期天跟一个朋友坐飞机去了中国？Who flew to China with a friend on Sunday?

6 几 (jǐ, question word)
几 can be used to ask about time, age, quantity, etc.

- 我们几点去市中心？When will we go to the city centre?
- 现在是几月？Which month is it?
- 今天星期几？What day is today?
- 您几岁了？How old are you?
- 你有几个苹果？How many apples have you got?

Practice text 7

玛雅现在是新加坡中文学校的交换学生。她从印尼来。她跟新加坡同学一起走路上学，每天都很忙，但是很高兴。早上她六点半起床，七点吃早餐，七点二十分就去学校，八点上课。上午的课很多，下午的课很少。玛雅学很多科目，她喜欢中文、数学和历史。学校每天五点才放学，非常晚。

玛雅的新学校很大，也很漂亮，有体育馆、礼堂和很多教室。她从小就想学中文，可是她在印尼的学校没有中文课，所以她现在才开始学中文。她天天跟新加坡同学一块儿说中文，也唱中文歌，已经会说很多了。

每天晚上，她上网跟印尼的朋友说英文，十点上床睡觉。

在周末玛雅喜欢坐地铁去市中心买东西，或去公园散步。

1 请阅读课文，选择正确的答案。Read the Practice text, and choose the only correct answer to each question.

i 玛雅在新加坡怎么去学校？

A 走路 **B** 跟老师一起 **C** 坐公共汽车

ii 玛雅几点吃早饭？

A 六点半 **B** 七点 **C** 七点二十

iii 她可以在哪儿看印尼的朋友？

A 上学 **B** 网上 **C** 市中心

iv 她周末去公园做什么？

A 买东西 **B** 睡觉 **C** 散步

2 请根据表格判断正误。Look at the table and answer the 'True' or 'False' questions in your exercise book.

小林的课表					
	星期一	星期二	星期三	星期四	星期五
9:00–10:00	英语	汉语	音乐	历史	数学
11:15–12:15	历史	画画	英语	数学	英语
2:30–3:30	网球	数学	汉语	唱歌	篮球

	是	非
i 小林没有化学课。	☐	☐
ii 小林每天都上数学课。	☐	☐
iii 小林星期一、星期四学历史。	☐	☐

3 小红在讲她在学校的一天。请听录音，选择正确的答案。Xiaohong is talking about her day at school. Listen to the recording and write down the correct answer according to the pictures.

i

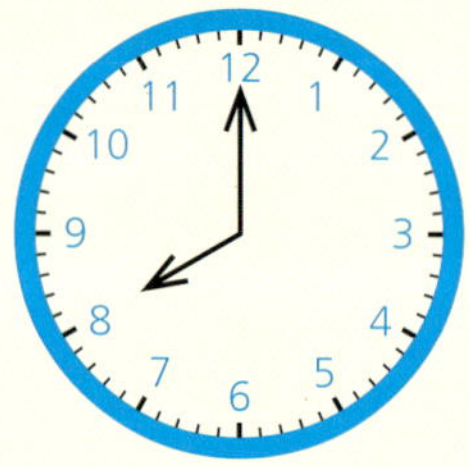

ii

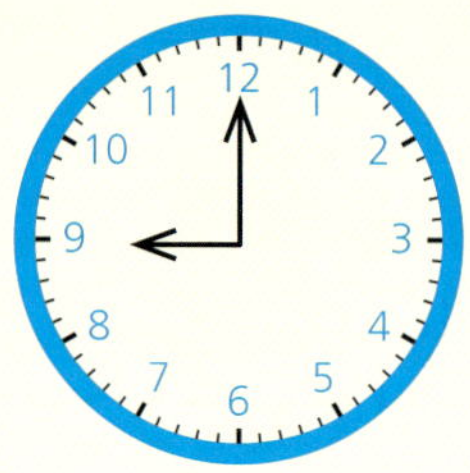
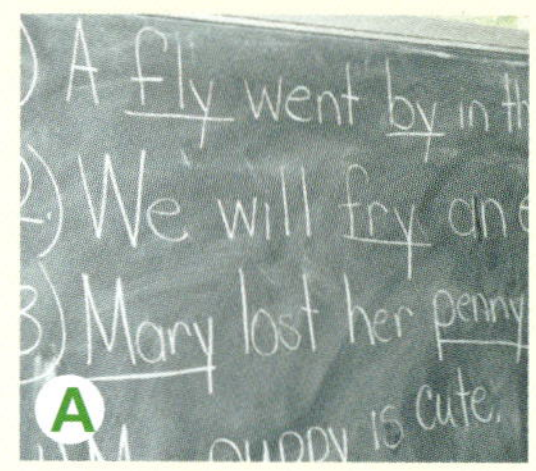

iii

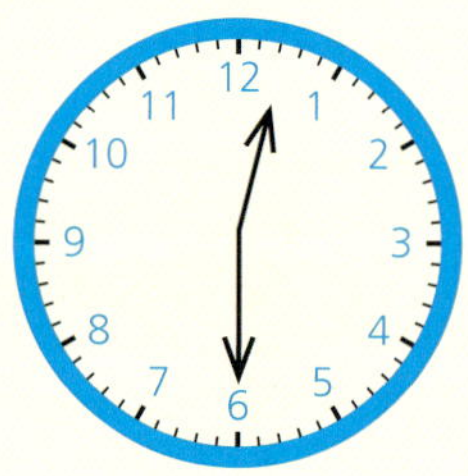

iv

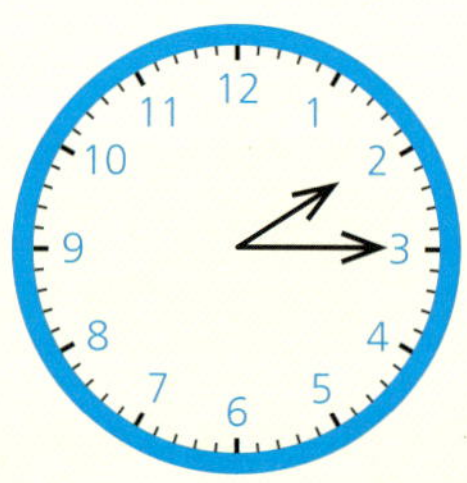

v

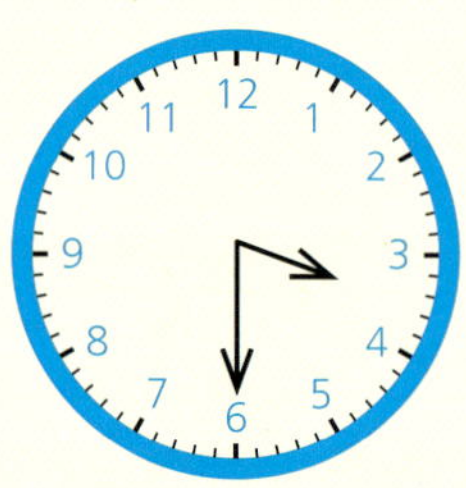

4 请用中文写出你在学校看到什么。Write in Chinese five things you see in a school.

5 学唱歌。Learn to sing in Chinese to the tune of *Frère Jacques* (*Are you sleeping?*). Use the words in the box below to help you.

Daily routine

měi tiān zǎo shang
每 天 早 上
qī diǎn qǐ chuáng
七 点 起 床
qī diǎn bàn chī zǎo fàn
七 点 半 吃 早 饭
bā diǎn bàn qù xué xiào
八 点 半 去 学 校
bā diǎn wǔ shí
八 点 五 十
kāi shǐ shàng kè
开 始 上 课
shàng wǔ yǒu sì jié kè
上 午 有 四 节 课
dōu xǐ huan
都 喜 欢
měi tiān wǎn shang
每 天 晚 上
liù diǎn chī wǎn fàn
六 点 吃 晚 饭
xīng qī yī kàn diàn shì
星 期 一 看 电 视
shí diǎn shuì jiào
十 点 睡 觉

měi tiān zǎo shang
每 天 早 上
qī diǎn qǐ chuáng
七 点 起 床
qī diǎn bàn chī zǎo fàn
七 点 半 吃 早 饭
bā diǎn bàn qù xué xiào
八 点 半 去 学 校
bā diǎn wǔ shí
八 点 五 十
kāi shǐ shàng kè
开 始 上 课
xià wǔ yǒu liǎng jié kè
下 午 有 两 节 课
dōu xǐ huan
都 喜 欢
měi tiān wǎn shang
每 天 晚 上
liù diǎn chī wǎn fàn
六 点 吃 晚 饭
xīng qī èr tīng yīn yuè
星 期 二 听 音 乐
shí diǎn shuì jiào
十 点 睡 觉

第八章 校园

Dialogue A

你在一家书店买学习用品。You are in a bookshop buying things you need for your studies. Your teacher acts as the shop assistant.

shī　nǐ yào mǎi shén me shū
师：你要买什么书？
nǐ　wǒ yào mǎi hàn yǔ kè běn hé cí diǎn
你：我要买汉语课本和词典。
shī　nǐ xiǎng mǎi jǐ běn
师：你想买几本？
nǐ　měi gè yì běn　hái yào liù zhī bǐ
你：每个一本，还要六支笔。
shī　nǐ xiǎng mǎi nǎ yì zhǒng bǐ
师：你想买哪一种笔？
nǐ　máo bǐ hé qiān bǐ　měi zhǒng yào sān zhī
你：毛笔和铅笔，每种要三支。
shī　nǐ hái yào shén me
师：你还要什么？
nǐ　wǒ kě yǐ kàn kan shū bāo ma　wǒ de shū bāo yǒu diǎnr jiù le
你：我可以看看书包吗？我的书包有点儿旧了。
shī　zhè ge shū bāo kě yǐ ma
师：这个书包可以吗？
nǐ　kě yǐ　wǒ yào zhè ge
你：可以，我要这个。

Dialogue B

你在学校的小卖部买文具。You are now in the school convenience store buying stationery. Your teacher acts as the shop assistant.

shī　nǐ xiǎng mǎi shén me
师：你想买什么？
nǐ　wǒ xiǎng mǎi wén jù　yì bǎ chǐ zi　liǎng kuài xiàng pí　yì zhī gāng bǐ
你：我想买文具：一把尺子、两块橡皮、一支钢笔、
yì zhī yuán zhū bǐ hé yì xiē zhǐ
一支圆珠笔和一些纸。
shī　nǐ yào mò shuǐr ma
师：你要墨水儿吗？
nǐ　bú yào　wǒ hái yào yí gè liàn xí běn
你：不要，我还要一个练习本。
shī　nǐ yào dà liàn xí běn hái shì xiǎo liàn xí běn
师：你要大练习本还是小练习本？
nǐ　xiǎo liàn xí běn
你：小练习本。
shī　hái yào shén me
师：还要什么？
nǐ　hái yào yì zhāng míng xìn piàn
你：还要一张明信片。
shī　yí gòng shí liù kuài wǔ máo　nǐ yǒu líng qián ma
师：一共十六块五毛。你有零钱吗？
nǐ　tài bù hǎo le　wǒ wàng jì wǒ de qián bāo le
你：太不好了！我忘记我的钱包了！

Vocabulary

chǐ zi	尺子	ruler	sù shè	宿舍	dormitory
bái bǎn	白板	whiteboard	xiǎo shuō	小说	novel/fiction
zhǐ	纸	paper	yǒu diǎnr yì diǎnr	有点儿/一点儿	a little
máo bǐ	毛笔	calligraphy pen	yì xiē	(一)些	some
qiān bǐ	铅笔	pencil	zhè xiē	这些	these
gāng bǐ	钢笔	fountain pen	duō shǎo	多少	how much/many
rì cháng yòng pǐn	日常用品	commodity	qián	钱	money
měi	每	every	líng qián	零钱	small change
yuán zhū bǐ	圆珠笔	Biro™	qián bāo	钱包	purse; wallet
mò shuǐr	墨水儿	ink	kuài yuán	块/元	(currency unit)
kè běn	课本	textbook	máo jiǎo	毛/角	(currency unit)
liàn xí běn	练习本	exercise book	hái	还	in addition; also
běn zi	本子	notebook	huā qián	花(钱)	to spend (money)
shū bāo	书包	school bag	yí gòng	一共	altogether
xué yuàn	学院	college	jīn	斤	(weight unit)
xiàng pí	橡皮	rubber	gōng jīn	公斤	kilogram
wén jù	文具	stationery	wàng wàng jì	忘/忘记	to forget
cí diǎn	词典	dictionary	tài le	太……了	extremely; too
xiǎo mài bù	小卖部	convenience store	xiào yuán	校园	campus
shè shī shè bèi	设施/设备	facilities	zhào piān	照片	photo
cāo qiú chǎng	操/球场	playground	pāi zhào	拍照	to take a photo
shí yàn shì	实验室	laboratory	zhào xiàng jī	照相机	camera
zuò shí yàn	(做)实验	(to do an) experiment	míng xìn piàn	明信片	postcard
shí táng	食堂	canteen			

Grammar

Tips

- The Chinese measure words (量词) are like the partitive nouns in English, e.g., three **bottles** of milk.
- Go to the Appendices and learn more about the quantifiers and measure words.

1 In Chinese, there is no plural form for nouns. Instead, a 'measure word' needs to be used in conjunction with a 'number' to indicate quantity. There are similar expressions also in English such as in 'a cup of tea' or 'three pieces of cakes'. Word order is: number + measure word + noun.

Examples:

A 本 (běn, for book):

一本书 one book　　五本书 five books

B 张 (zhāng, with flat surfaces):

一张桌子 one table　　十张桌子 ten tables

2 二 (èr) and 两 (liǎng)

In phone numbers, door numbers, days and dates, page numbers and so on, 二 is used. However, 两 is used for telling the time, money, weights and ages, accompanied by a measure word.

现在两点 It is two o'clock now.　　两只狗 two dogs

3 一点儿 (yì diǎnr, a little) and 一些 (yì xiē, some)

一点儿 and 一些 are similar to English quantifiers, such as some, a little, and they do not specify exact quantities.

- 我要一点儿水。I would like to have a little bit of water.
- 妈妈买了一些点心。Mother bought some pastry.

Sometimes 一 can be omitted.

- 我有个朋友。I have a friend.
- 你们买了些什么？What did you buy?
- 我想看点儿书。I want to read something.

4 有点儿 (yǒu diǎnr, a little bit)

有点儿 is used to modify adjectives, telling the degree of a situation.

- 书包有点儿旧。The school bag is a little bit worn.
- 今天有点儿冷。Today is a little cold.
- 妈妈有点儿累。Mother is a little bit tired.

5 这/这些 (zhè, zhè xiē) and 那/那些 (nà, nà xiē)

These are similar to this/these and that/those in English in meaning and usage. 这/那 are followed by measure words or 点儿.

这本书 this book　　那条裙子 that skirt

这些老师 these teachers　　那些学生 those students

6 Plural forms

Singular	+ 们	+ (一)些	+/measure word
你 you	你们 you		
我 I	我们 we		
他 he	他们 they		
它 it	它们 they		
这 this		这些 these	这两人 these two people
那 that		那些 those	那三条鱼 those three fish
学生 student	学生们 students	这些/那些/一些学生 these/those/some students	五个学生 five students
书 book		这些/那些/一些书 these/those/some books	三本书 three books
桌子 table		这些/那些/一些桌子 these/those/some tables	十张桌子 ten tables

7 Asking about quantity
The rule is simple: replace the number with 几 (jǐ, how much/many).

- 王太太有几个孩子？How many children does Mrs Wang have?
  王太太有一个孩子。Mrs Wang has one child.

Tip

When asking about belongings, replace this or that with 哪 (nǎ, which).

哪本词典是你的？

这本词典是我的。

8 Ordinal numbers
Ordinal numbers are made up with 第 (dì) + a number.

第一 first　　第二 second　　第三 third

An ordinal number and a measure word are required to modify a noun.

- 这是我的第一节中文课。This is my first Chinese lesson.
- 第三个房间是我的卧室。The third room is my bedroom.

9 这儿/这里 (zhèr/zhè lǐ, here/in this place) and 那儿/那里 (nàr/nà lǐ, there/in that place)
These words can accompany a pronoun or noun to indicate a specific place.

- 杂志不在我这儿，在李校长那儿。The magazine is not with me (in my place), but with Headmaster Li (in his/her place).
- 我去朋友那里看电视，因为我这里没有电视。I will go to my friend's place to watch TV, because I don't have a TV at mine.

10 人民币 (rén mín bì, RMB)

A Chinese currency is called 人民币 and there are three units: 块/元, 角/毛 and 分. There are two names for the first two units in Chinese currency: 块 and 毛 for spoken language and 元 and 角 for written language; however, this rule is not observed strictly, so you can use either.

	£1.00 / ¥1.00	£0.10 / ¥0.10	£0.01 / ¥0.01
英镑 British pound	1 pound	10 pence	1 penny
人民币 Ren Min Bi	1 块 / 1 元	1 毛 / 1 角	1 分

1 pound = 100 pence

1 块/1 元 = 10 毛/10 角 = 100 分

B As you can see, there is no equivalent in English currency to 毛/角.

¥1.23 = 一块两毛三分 or 一元两角三分 ('and' is not used when talking about money)

C Sometimes you can omit 毛/角 or 分.

¥3.40 = 三块四毛 or 三块四 ¥6.45 = 六元四角五分 or 六元四角五

D If the middle unit is a zero, it must be mentioned.

¥89.07 = 八十九块零七分 or 八十九块零七

11 怎么卖 (zěn me mài, how is it sold) and 多少钱 (duō shǎo qián, how much money)

怎么卖 and 多少钱 are question words for asking the price. In Chinese, the question words or the price always come after the name of the goods/items or 一共 (altogether), with '一/每 + unit/measure word'.

- How much are the apples?

  苹果怎么卖? 苹果多少钱一斤? 一斤苹果多少钱? 苹果一斤多少钱?

  The apples are ten yuan per half a kilogram.

  苹果十元一斤。 一斤苹果十元。 苹果每斤十元。

- How much is it altogether?

  一共多少钱?

  It is altogether a hundred and twenty yuan.

  一共一百二十元。

Practice text 8

诺亚：

你好！

你想知道我在新加坡学校的日常生活吗？我现在就说说。

我们学校叫新风女子中学。校园很大，风景非常美。学校有一千五百多个学生，不只有新加坡学生，也有中国和马来西亚学生。校园里边有很多新设施，宿舍、教室、电脑室、小卖部都有。我们有两个食堂，一个大的，一个小的。校园中间是大操场，操场旁边还有一个足球场。我们教室后边就是实验室，我很喜欢在那里做实验。

我每天都去小卖部买日常用品跟学习用品，已经花了很多钱。昨天我在那里买了小白板、中文小说和本子。这些东西都不很贵。那儿也卖蛋糕，我昨天买了三斤蛋糕！我还想明天去市中心买一部照相机，可以拍很多照片，明年回印尼给你看。好了，不多说了！

你的朋友

玛雅

1 请阅读课文，然后回答问题。Read the Practice text, and then answer the questions.

i 新风女子中学的风景怎么样？

ii 学校有多少学生？

iii 校园里边有几个食堂？

iv 玛雅为什么喜欢去实验室？

v 学校的小卖部哪些东西便宜？（举出两个例子。）

vi 玛雅想去市中心做什么？为什么？

Tip

Time to revise these words!

dōng 东	xī 西	nán 南	běi 北
dōng biān 东边	xī biān 西边	nán biān 南边	běi biān 北边
dōng nán 东南	dōng běi 东北	xī nán 西南	xī běi 西北

2 你来到新学校，你的新同学给你介绍校园。请看图片。You have arrived at your new school and your new classmate talks to you about the school campus. Look at the pictures.

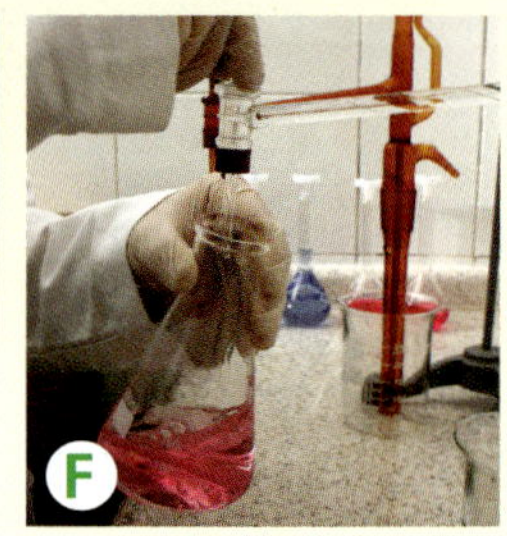

请听录音，将图片的字母分别填入适当的方格内。Listen, and put the correct letter in the appropriate box.

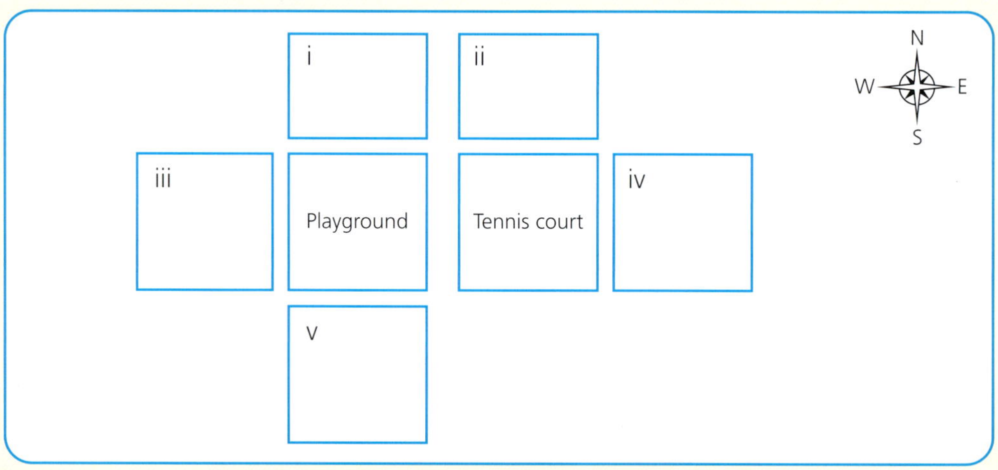

3 请用中文写出你在学校小卖部看到的东西。Write in Chinese five things you see in a school convenience store.

4 扩展练习。Look at the example questions and answers below, then write out your own answers to the question given, using the suggestions provided. This exercise can also be used for speaking practice.

	Question	Sample answers
Examples:	你的新家怎么样？ What is your new house like?	• 我的新家很大很漂亮。 • 有很多房间和一个花园，也有一个大厨房和两个卫生间。我都喜欢。 • 客厅里有电视，我们天天晚上看电视。 • 花园里有很多花，我妈妈爱花。 • 我的卧室大，也舒服，弟弟的卧室小。 • 我喜欢饭厅，因为那儿有好吃的。
	你的新朋友怎么样？ What is your new friend like?	• 我有很多新朋友。 • 我有英国朋友，也有中国朋友。 • 他们都很友好，常常跟我一起做运动。 • 我每天早上跟他们一起去学校。 • 他们有很多爱好。 • 我喜欢这些朋友。
You do it:	你的新学校怎么样？ What is your new school like?	• My new school is very big and very beautiful. • There are many classrooms and a big assembly hall. • There are many computer rooms and two libraries, one big, one small. • I often go to the sportsground. • I like to play football with my new classmates. • I learn many subjects: English, Chinese, History. I like them all.

5 你的奶奶想知道你的新学校。请给她写一封150字左右的信。信里说：
Your grandma wants to know what your new school is like. Write her a letter of about 150 Chinese characters and say:

- 你们的校园怎么样；
- 都有什么设施；
- 你都学些什么科目；
- 你的新同学怎么样；
- 上个周末你去哪儿了。

第九章 学生的生活

Dialogue A

今天一位中国老师来你的学校跟你说中文。Today a Chinese teacher has come to your school and is talking to you in Chinese.

shī nǐ duō dà le
师：你多大了？
nǐ wǒ jīn nián shí wǔ suì
你：我今年十五岁。
shī nǐ de shēng rì shì jǐ yuè jǐ hào
师：你的生日是几月几号？
nǐ liù yuè wǔ hào
你：六月五号。
shī nǐ men xué xiào yì nián yǒu jǐ gè xué qī
师：你们学校一年有几个学期？
nǐ wǒ men yǒu sān gè xué qī qiū jì chūn jì hé xià jì
你：我们有三个学期：秋季、春季和夏季。
shī nǐ men dōu yǒu shén me cháng jià qī
师：你们都有什么长假期？
nǐ shǔ jià yǒu yí gè duō yuè chūn jià yǒu liǎng gè xīng qī zuǒ yòu
你：暑假有一个多月，春假有两个星期左右。
shī nǐ men shén me shí hou fàng shǔ jià
师：你们什么时候放暑假？
nǐ qī yuè èr shí hào qián hòu fàng jià
你：七月二十号前后放假。

Dialogue B

你带一位新来的中文老师去校长的办公室，你跟他说中文。You are taking your new Chinese teacher to the headmaster's office and are talking to him in Chinese.

shī nǐ lái zhè ge xué xiào shàng xué yǐ jīng duō jiǔ le
师：你来这个学校上学已经多久了？
nǐ liǎng nián le
你：两年了。
shī nǐ xué le duō cháng shí jiān de hàn yǔ
师：你学了多长时间的汉语？
nǐ liù gè yuè
你：六个月。
shī nǐ wèi shén me xué hàn yǔ
师：你为什么学汉语？
nǐ wǒ xiǎng qù zhōng guó gōng zuò tiān tiān chī zhōng guó fàn
你：我想去中国工作，天天吃中国饭。
shī nǐ huì cān jiā xià gè xīng qī de zhōng wén chàng gē bǐ sài ma
师：你会参加下个星期的中文唱歌比赛吗？
nǐ bú huì yīn wèi wǒ de zhōng wén hái bú shì hěn hǎo
你：不会，因为我的中文还不是很好。
shī xiào zhǎng de bàn gōng shì zài nǎr
师：校长的办公室在哪儿？
nǐ jiù zài qián biān
你：就在前边。

Vocabulary

kè chéng 课程	curriculum
kè chéng biǎo 课程表	lesson table
shí jiān biǎo 时间表	timetable
xué qī 学期	school term
jià qī 假期	holiday
fàng 放	to place; to put
fàng jià 放假	to be on holiday
nián jí 年级	grade; year group
jiā zhǎng 家长	parent
jiā zhǎng huì 家长会	parent's meeting
liú xué shēng 留学生	overseas student
xiǎo xué 小学	primary school
zhōng xué 中学	secondary school
dà xué 大学	university
yuè 月	month
rì hào 日/号	day of the month
rì qī 日期	date
de shí hou 的时候	while; when
yǐ qián 以前	previously; before
yǐ hòu 以后	after
zhù 住	to live (in)
bǐ sài 比赛	competition
cān jiā 参加	to take part in
liàn xí 练习	exercise; practice
jié shù 结束	to end; to finish
lí kāi 离开	to leave
zuì hòu 最后	lastly; last
cháng 长	long
duǎn 短	short (length)
fù xí 复习	to revise
suì 岁	... years old
xiǎo shí 小时	hour
zuǒ yòu 左右	approximately
chà bu duō 差不多	more or less
shēng rì 生日	birthday
shí jiān 时间	time
shén me shí hou 什么时候	what time; when
jì jié 季节	season
chūn tiān chūn jì 春天/春季	spring
xià tiān xià jì 夏天/夏季	summer
qiū tiān qiū jì 秋天/秋季	autumn
dōng tiān dōng jì 冬天/冬季	winter
bái tiān tiān 白天/天	daytime
yè lǐ yè 夜里/夜	night-time
míng xiào 名校	famous university
yòu ér yuán 幼儿园	nursery
bàn gōng shì 办公室	office
xiào zhǎng 校长	head of school
yǒu yì si yǒu qù 有意思/有趣	interesting
méi yì si méi qù 没意思/没趣	boring
zuò yè 作业	prep; homework
chú le yǐ wài hái 除了……以外(还)	besides; apart from
yì si 意思	meaning
bāo 包	bag; packet

Grammar

1 Talking about time and date

Time	One before last	Last / previous	This	Next / following	One after next
月	上上个月	上个月	这个月	下个月	下下个月
星期	上上个星期	上个星期	这个星期	下个星期	下下个星期
年	前年	去年	今年	明年	后年
天	前天	昨天	今天	明天	后天

A Word order for dates

The word order for dates is 年 + 月 + 日 (largest unit first) as in 一九九七年一月六日(号). For 'years', the numbers are read in single digits and the number 'zero' needs to be read as 零. So if you want to say '3:05 pm on 6th July 2015', the correct way to write it is 2015年7月6号下午 3:05, and it reads 二零一五年七月六号下午三点零五分.

Tip

There is little difference between 日 and 号 in dates, but 号 can also be used for counting numbers as in 五号门 (door Number 5) or 六号窗 (window Number 6).

B Difference between a length of time and a point in time

	Year	Month	Week	Day	Hour	Minute
A point in time	今年 this year 明年 next year	一月 January 二月 February	星期一 Monday 星期二 Tuesday	今天 today 明天 tomorrow	五点 5:00	二十分 twenty minutes (past etc.)
A length of time	一年 one year 两年 two years	一个月 one month 两个月 two months	一个星期 one week 两个星期 two weeks	一天 one day 两天 two days	五个小时 five hours	二十分钟 twenty minutes

2 Sometimes verbs can be omitted, for example, when talking about age.

- 您多大了？How old are you?
  我六十岁。I am sixty (years old).
- 他几岁？How old is he?
  他十五岁。He is fifteen (years old).

- 今天星期六。Today is Saturday. (今天是星期六。)
- 他法国人。He is French. (他是法国人。)
- 一节课四十五分钟。One lesson has/is/lasts for forty-five minutes. (一节课有/是四十五分钟。)

3 To be less specific when referring to age, timing or quantity, you can use phrases like 差不多 (more or less) or phrases involving direction and position words 上下, 左右, 前后, which mean 'thereabouts'. If you want to say 'several', you can use 几 instead of giving a number.

A When talking about age:

- 哥哥三十六、七岁。My elder brother is about thirty-six or thirty-seven years old.
- 我的妹妹差不多二十了。My younger sister is nearly twenty years old.

B When talking about time or a period of time:

- 他来英国有几个月了。It has been several months since he came to the UK.
- 差不多春天了。It is nearly spring now.
- 我们暑假前后出发。We will set off around the summer holidays.

C When talking about surroundings:

- 这边左右都是树。It is all trees around here.
- 我家前后都是山。My home is sandwiched between mountains.

D Talking about quantity:

- 我买了六、七本书。I bought six or seven books.

4 Question words can be formed with 多少 + noun (measure words are optional).

	How much money	How many people	How many days	How many weeks	How many chairs	How many minutes	How many hours
With 多少	多少钱	多少人	多少天	多少个星期	多少椅子	多少分钟	多少个小时
With 几	几元	几个人	几天	几个星期	几把椅子	几分钟	几个小时

Question words can also be formed using 多 + adjective.

多大 how old	多高 how tall	多长 how long	多重 how heavy
多远 how far	多近 how close	多久 how long (time)	多深 how deep

So there are different ways to ask a question:

- How old are you?
  你几岁？/你多大？
- How long does one lesson last?
  一节课多长时间？/一节课多久/一节课多少分钟？

5 时间 (shí jiān, length of time)
and 时候 (shí hou, a point in time)
时间 and 时候 both mean 'time' but 时间 refers to duration/length of time, while 时候 refers to a point in time; hence they require different question words/phrases: 'how long in time' for 多长时间, while 'what time/when' for 什么时候.

Tip

Watch out! Sometimes they swap roles but only in certain circumstances, for example announcing the time.

现在是北京时间十四点整。

- 你有时间吗？Do you have time (to spare)?
- 你什么时候出发？When do you set off?

6 ……的时候 (de shí hou, while)
Unlike 什么时候 used for asking about time, 的时候 is similar to the English 'while' and needs something before it.

- 上课的时候 while having lessons/in lesson time
- 春天的时候 while in spring/in spring time

7 会 (huì, most likely) and 要 (yào, will/want to)

A 会 and 要 are two characters which are similar to the English future tense as they emphasize on something that is almost certainly going to happen.

- 明天朋友要来看我。Tomorrow, my friend will (want to) come and see me.
- 明天会下雪。It will (most likely) snow tomorrow.

B To express that something is unlikely to happen, use 不会 because 不要 has a different meaning of 'refusing to'.

- 明天朋友不会来看我。My friend will not come to see me.
- 明天不会下雪。 It will not snow tomorrow.

C To say that something is very soon or sure to take place, 快要……了, 要……了 or 快……了 can be used.

- 我快十六岁了。I am going to be sixteen soon.
- 家长会快要开始了。The parent's meeting is going to start soon.
- 要热了。It is going to get hot soon.

Practice text 9

黄波今年十六岁，是北京中学三年级的学生。他的学校有很多留学生，可是黄波没有时间跟他们一起玩儿，因为课程太多了！他的时间表上差不多每个小时都有课；中午也要学音乐或者画画，只有十分钟的时间吃午餐；放学后还要练足球或者参加比赛，这些活动常常晚上八点才结束。晚饭以后，除了写作业以外，他还要复习，最后只能睡五、六个小时。真是很忙！

在上个周末的家长会上，校长跟他妈妈说黄波应该少做一些活动。可是妈妈说多学东西，才能上名校。

快要放暑假了，黄波想离开家去香港一所幼儿园工作一个月，时间不长也不短，不住在家里，应该非常有意思！

1 请阅读课文，选择正确的答案。Read the Practice text, and choose the only correct answer to each question.

i 黄波没有时间跟留学生在一起，是因为：

A 他们不会说汉语。

B 他要学太多科目。

C 他不想吃午餐。

ii 黄波每天可以睡多长时间？

A 八个小时左右

B 差不多六个小时

C 两个小时

iii 妈妈说黄波想上好大学，得做什么？

A 去香港。

B 少做活动。

C 学很多东西。

iv 为什么黄波说幼儿园的工作会有意思？

A 因为他喜欢香港。

B 因为他可以少做活动。

C 这段时间他不住在家里。

2 小李在讲她跟哥哥的一天。请听对话，并选择正确的答案回答问题。
Xiao Li talks about her day wth her brother. Listen, and choose the correct letter for each question.

i

ii

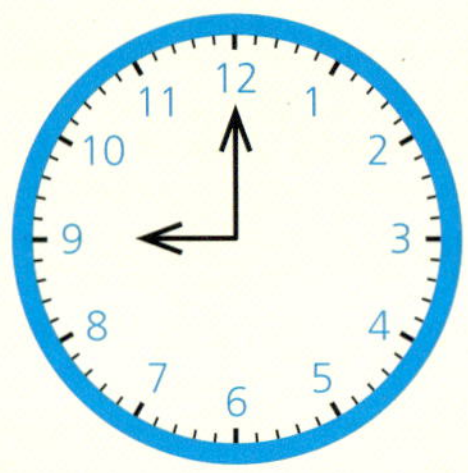

iii

iv

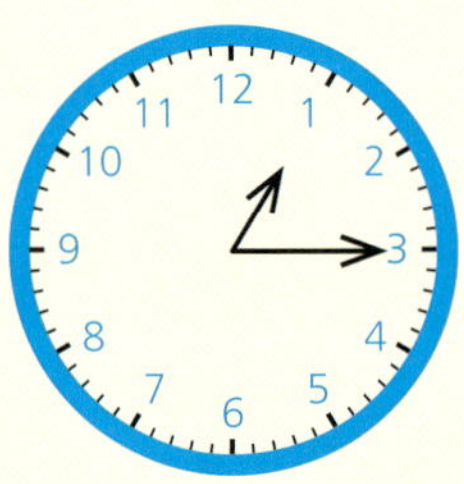

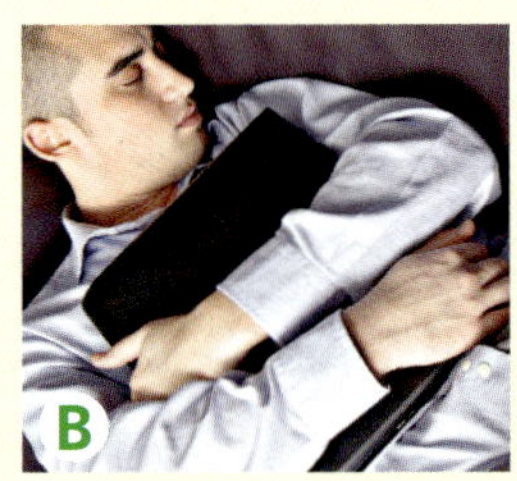

v

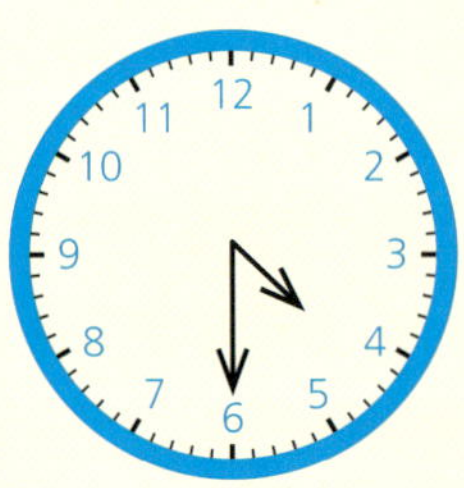

3 请听对一名中国留学生的采访，用中文或拼音回答问题。Listen to an interview with a Chinese student studying abroad and answer the questions in Chinese. You may write your answers in Chinese characters or Pinyin.

i 赵云在新加坡几年了？

ii 赵云怎么去学校？

[PAUSE]

iii 赵云说在新加坡留学有哪些好处 (benefit)？

iv 她在大学想学习什么专业？

4 扩展练习。Look at the example question and answers below, then write out your own answers to the question given, using the suggestions provided. This exercise can also be used for speaking practice.

	Question	**Sample answers**
Example:	你喜欢什么课？ What lessons do you like?	• 我喜欢很多科目。 • 中文、物理、生物，我都喜欢。 • 除了中文以外，我还喜欢法文。 • 因为我想去法国，所以我学法文。 • 生物课没有很多作业，所以我喜欢生物。 • 英文很有意思，所以我每天都看英文书。 • 我也爱看英文电影。 • 我常常在周末去电影院看英文电影。
You do it:	你想学什么科目？ What subjects do you want to study?	• I want to learn many subjects. • Chinese, History, English, I want to learn them all. • Apart from Geography, I also want to learn Maths. • I like little animals, so I want to learn Biology. • Chinese is very interesting, so I want to learn Chinese. • I also want to go to China.

5 请给你的中国笔友写一封100–150字的信，信里说：Write to your Chinese penfriend a letter of 100–150 Chinese characters and say:

- 你的学校有多少学生；
- 你是几年级的学生；
- 你怎么去学校；
- 你喜欢什么课；
- 你在大学想学什么科目，为什么。

第十章 你喜欢什么科目

Dialogue A

你在一所中学跟一位从中国来的汉语老师谈你的学习。You are talking to a Chinese teacher who has come from China about your studies.

shī　nǐ xǐ huan shàng shén me kè
师：你喜欢上什么课？
nǐ　wǒ xǐ huan shàng shēng wù měi shù hé tǐ yù
你：我喜欢上生物、美术和体育。
shī　nǐ jǐ nián jí kāi shǐ xué shēng wù
师：你几年级开始学生物？
nǐ　sān nián jí
你：三年级。
shī　nǐ yí gè xīng qī yǒu jǐ jié měi shù kè
师：你一个星期有几节美术课？
nǐ　sì jié
你：四节。
shī　jiāo nǐ měi shù de lǎo shī xìng shén me
师：教你美术的老师姓什么？
nǐ　tā xìng zhào
你：他姓赵。
shī　zhào lǎo shī shì yí gè shén me yàng de lǎo shī
师：赵老师是一个什么样的老师？
nǐ　tā hěn gāo hěn yǒu hǎo měi tiān dōu hěn kāi xīn
你：他很高，很友好，每天都很开心。

Dialogue B

你跟校长谈你的汉语学习。You are talking to your headmaster about your Chinese studies.

xiào zhǎng　nǐ de hàn yǔ shì shuí jiāo de
校长：你的汉语是谁教的？
nǐ　liú lǎo shī
你：刘老师。
xiào zhǎng　hàn yǔ nán xué ma
校长：汉语难学吗？
nǐ　wǒ jué de bú tài róng yì kě shì hěn yǒu qù
你：我觉得不太容易，可是很有趣。
xiào zhǎng　shàng kè de shí hou nǐ men shuō pǔ tōng huà ma
校长：上课的时候你们说普通话吗？
nǐ　yǒu shí hou shuō pǔ tōng huà yǒu shí hou shuō yīng yǔ
你：有时候说普通话，有时候说英语。
xiào zhǎng　nǐ huì xiě duō shǎo hàn zì
校长：你会写多少汉字？
nǐ　bù duō wǒ zhī huì xiě yì bǎi duō gè hàn zì
你：不多，我只会写一百多个汉字。
xiào zhǎng　nǐ de zhōng guó péng you bāng nǐ liàn xí hàn yǔ ma
校长：你的中国朋友帮你练习汉语吗？
nǐ　tā men jiāo wǒ zuò nà xiē wǒ bú huì zuò de nán tí
你：他们教我做那些我不会做的难题。

Vocabulary

kǎo kǎo shì	考/考试	to take an exam; exam
yǔ yán	语言	language
wài yǔ wài wén	外语/外文	foreign language
pǔ tōng huà guó yǔ	普通话/国语	Mandarin
fǎ yǔ fǎ wén	法语/法文	French
dé yǔ dé wén	德语/德文	German
rì yǔ rì wén	日语/日文	Japanese
kē xué	科学	Science
huà xué	化学	Chemistry
shēng wù	生物	Biology
wù lǐ	物理	Physics
měi shù yì shù	美术/艺术	Art
tǐ yù	体育	PE
dì lǐ	地理	Geography
nán kùn nan	难/困难	difficult; difficulty
róng yì	容易	easy
bù yí dìng	不一定	not necessarily
yì zhí	一直	all along; always
chéng jì	成绩	achievement
duì gǎn xìng qù	对……感兴趣	to be interested in
cuò cuò wù	错/错误	wrong; mistake
bú cuò	不错	correct; not bad
chà	差	to lack; lacking; bad
jué de	觉得	to feel; to think
rèn wéi	认为	to believe; to think
dǎ suàn	打算	to plan; to intend
zhǔn bèi	准备	to prepare

liàn xí	练习	practice; exercise
jiào yù	教育	education
jiào xué jiāo shū	教学/教书	teaching
ér tóng	儿童	child
wèn tí	问题	problem; question
nǔ lì	努力	hardworking
rèn zhēn	认真	conscientious
jiāo tōng	交通	transport
fāng shì fāng fǎ	方式/方法	method
xiě	写	to write
xìn	信	letter
tán huà	谈话	to chat
hàn zì	汉字	written Chinese words
jiāo liú	交流	communication
yǒu shí hou	有时候	sometimes
cōng míng	聪明	intelligent
yòng yǒu yòng	用/有用	to use; useful
zhù dú	住读	to be a boarder
zǒu dú	走读	to be a day student
fāng biàn	方便	convenient
bāng bāng zhù	帮/帮助	to help
shén me yàng de	什么样的	what sort of?
guò	过	to pass; (particle)
cóng qián	从前	in the past
zhǎo	找	to look for
gǎn	敢	to dare

Grammar

1 When 的 is used to form a link between parts of a sentence, the second part is sometimes referred to as a 'subordinate'. When this happens, we call it a 'complex sentence with a subordinate clause'. A scary-looking title indeed! However, it is not as difficult to form as it seems and it is actually a very useful sentence structure!

Simple sentence:	Sentence with a clause:
I like to eat fish.	I like to eat the fish (that) my mother cooks.

The two sentences above are more or less the same, except more information about the fish is provided; 'that my mother cooks' in this situation is 'the subordinate'. Subordinate clauses give more information about nouns; in other words they modify them.

Here are some more examples:

- The things (that/which) she loves buying are all expensive.
- This is the teacher who teaches me chemistry.
- The day (when) we went to the park was very hot.
- I know the gym where he often goes to swim.
- The book (that) he gave me is very interesting.

In these complex sentences, 'which', 'when', 'where', 'who', and 'that' are used to modify the nouns before them. Let's call them 'markers'. These markers are not always used in English, and when you translate these sentences into Chinese, you must leave the markers out.

Identify the marker and underline the words on either side of it to separate the clauses, like this:

- The things **which** she loves buying are all expensive.
- This is the teacher **who** teaches me chemistry.
- The day **when** we went to the park was very hot.
- I know the gym **where** he often goes to swim.
- The book **that** he gave me is very interesting.

Next, swap the two parts that have been underlined but **leave the rest of the sentence where it is**, like this:

- she loves buying **which** The things are all expensive.
- This is teaches me chemistry **who** the teacher.
- we went to the park **when** The day was very hot.
- I know he often goes to swim **where** the gym
- he gave me **that** The book is very interesting.

In Chinese, you can replace all these markers with 的. Now you can begin:

- 她喜欢买 的 东西都贵。
- 这是教我化学 的 老师。
- 我们去公园 的 那天很热。
- 我知道他常去游泳 的 体育馆。
- 他给我 的 书很有意思。

Now translate them back into English using the same procedure in reverse. Your translation should match the original sentences.

- 她喜欢买的东西都贵。
- 这是教我化学的老师。
- 我们去公园的那天很热。
- 我知道他常去游泳的体育馆。
- 他给我的书很有意思。

Tips

- In Chinese, there is no equivalent word for 'the'. You must convert 'the' to 'this' or 'that' when translating.
- Flexibility is required when translating complex sentences:
  我有很多学习中文的好方法。
  I have many good methods for learning Chinese.

2 In Chinese, the words for some professions and careers are formed by adding 的. For example, 卖报 (selling newspapers) becomes 卖报的 (newspaper seller).

卖鱼的	fishmonger
送报的	paper delivery boy
看门的	doorman/guard
开车的	driver/chauffeur

Tip

You don't need 人 in this case.

These noun phrases can be used the same way as nouns but, when translating into English, additional words should be added, such as 'the … one(s)/thing(s)'.

- 大的六块，小的两块。The big one costs six yuan, and the small one costs two yuan.
- 我要贵的，他要便宜的。I want the expensive one, and he wants the cheap one.

This structure is very useful for shortening sentences:

- 我妈妈喜欢吃辣的，爸爸喜欢吃咸的，爷爷喜欢吃酸的，奶奶喜欢吃苦的，姐姐喜欢吃甜的，我咸的、辣的、甜的、酸的、苦的，都爱吃。
  My mum likes spicy (food), dad likes salty (food), grandpa likes sour (food), grandma likes bitter (food), and my elder sister likes sweet things. As for me, spicy, salty, sweet, sour and bitter, I like them all.

3 To highlight aspects of past events, use 是……的.

A To highlight when:

- 他**是什么时候**去**的**北京？When was it that he went to Beijing?

B To highlight with whom:

- 你**是跟朋友**去中国**的**吗？Did you go to China with friends?

C To highlight where:

- 妹妹的本子**是在书店**买**的**。My sister's notebook was bought in the bookshop.

D To highlight how:

- 李太太**是坐飞机**去美国**的**。Mrs Li went to the USA by air.

4 In Chinese, when we want to give negative opinions such as 'I don't think/believe/feel that ...', we do not use the word 不 before the verbs 'to think', 'to believe' and 'to feel'. Instead, 不 goes with the main verb in the sentence.

- 我认为他不是一个喜欢科学的人。I don't think he is a person who likes science.
- 老师们认为学生们不应该只学习，不休息。Teachers don't think students should only study without rest.

Practice text 10

小赵：

你好！

我们快要考试了，所以我每天都很忙。

我最喜欢学的科目是语言，打算明年去南京大学学法文和日文。可是不会很容易，因为想去这所名校的同学太多了，都想找能用外语的工作。我认为我不太聪明，但是学习方法不算差，而且我天天认真努力，希望能有好成绩。

以前我是走读生。因为我家不在学校旁边，交通也不便利。今年，我开始住读了。有困难的时候，跟同学谈话很方便。有了问题，就跟老师交流，很不错。

儿童教学是我朋友李新很想做的工作。他的考试成绩一直不错。他爸爸是科学家，昨天从工作了六个月的上海回来帮助他准备数学考试。可是他对科学不感兴趣，可是不敢告诉他爸爸。我们都觉得很有意思。

你的朋友

小王

1 请阅读课文，然后回答问题。Read the Practice text, and then answer the questions.

i 小王为什么很忙？

ii 他想去什么大学？

iii 小王的学习怎么样？(举出两个例子)

iv 他现在住在哪儿？

v 他家到学校的交通怎么样？

vi 李新想做什么工作？

vii 他爸爸在哪儿工作？

2 朋友们一起谈他们离开中学以后的打算。请看图片。Some friends are talking about what they plan to do after they leave high school. Look at the pictures.

请听录音，选择正确的图片回答问题。Listen, and for each person choose the correct picture.

i 兰花 **ii** 东东 **iii** 小京 **iv** 小海 **v** 小红

3 请听对一名高中生的采访，用中文或拼音回答问题。Listen to an interview with a high school student and answer the questions. You may write your answers in Chinese characters or Pinyin.

i 记者为什么采访 (interview) 刘月？

ii 刘月的爸爸做什么工作？

[PAUSE]

iii 刘月用的学习方法都有哪些？

iv 周末的下午，他去公园做什么？

4 记住下面的短语。Treat the following phrases as individual words and learn them by heart.

Learn as words	English
妈妈做的菜	the dish that my mother cooked
爸爸给我的礼物	the gift which my father gave me
我住的地方	the place where I live
他去北京的那天	the day when he went to Beijing

请将下列句子翻译成中文。Translate the English sentences into Chinese using the words provided below, and write them in your exercise book.

喜欢	爱	星期天	好吃	安静

A Everyone likes the dish (that) my mother cooked.
B I love the gift (that) my father gave me.
C He does not like the place where I live.
D The day when he went to Beijing was a Sunday.
E The dish (which) my mother cooked is delicious.
F The place where I live is very quiet.

5 扩展练习。Look at the example question and answers below, then write out your own answers to the question given, using the suggestions provided. This exercise can also be used for speaking practice.

	Question	Sample answers
Example:	你是什么时候开始学唱歌的？When did you begin learning to sing?	• 我很小的时候就喜欢唱歌。 • 我在小学一年级的时候开始学唱歌。 • 开始的时候我觉得唱歌很难。 • 唱德文歌很难。 • 因为我家人不会德文，不能帮助我。 • 虽然难，可是我觉得唱歌很有意思，所以想学。
You do it:	你觉得什么科目难？What subject do you think is the hardest?	• I think English is very difficult. • My family do not speak English, so they cannot help me. • I have many methods for learning English. • I listen to English songs and speak English with my classmates every day. • Writing in English is not difficult, but writing Chinese characters is very difficult. • Although English is very difficult, I want to study English in university. I love English.

6 你的校长想调查在校生学习的情况。请给他/她写一封150字左右的信，信里说：Your school headmaster wants to know how students are getting on with their studies. Write a letter of about 150 Chinese characters to him/her and say:

- 你是几年级开始学中文的；
- 你觉得什么科目难/容易；
- 你学习中文的方法有哪些；
- 你喜欢学中文吗，为什么；
- 以后你打算用中文做些什么。

第十一章 饮食

Dialogue A

你跟中国朋友在一家中国饭馆吃饭。跟在那里工作的服务员说话。You are having a meal with Chinese friends in a Chinese restaurant, and are talking to the waitress there.

fú wù yuán　nǐ hē shén me yǐn liào
服务员：你喝什么饮料？

nǐ　wǒ men hē kā fēi　guǒ zhī hé shuǐ ba
你：我们喝咖啡、果汁和水吧。

fú wù yuán　nǐ yào chī nǎ zhǒng cài
服务员：你要吃哪种菜？

nǐ　wǒ yào chī kǎo yā　jī hé niú ròu miàn
你：我要吃烤鸭、鸡和牛肉面。

fú wù yuán　yào mǐ fàn ma
服务员：要米饭吗？

nǐ　bú yào　wǒ yào bāo zi
你：不要，我要包子。

fú wù yuán　nǐ xiǎng chī shén me yàng de　niú ròu de hái shì yáng ròu de
服务员：你想吃什么样的？牛肉的还是羊肉的？

nǐ　nǐ shuō nǎ yì zhǒng hǎo　nǐ yǐ qián chī guò yáng ròu bāo zi méi yǒu
你：你说哪一种好？你以前吃过羊肉包子没有？

fú wù yuán　chī guò　hěn hǎo chī　nǐ men hái yào tāng ma
服务员：吃过，很好吃。你们还要汤吗？

nǐ　yào yí gè hǎi xiān tāng
你：要一个海鲜汤。

Dialogue B

你跟朋友做了一个小时的运动，准备去吃饭。You have just done one hour of sport with your friend and are going to have something to eat.

péng you　nǐ zhōng wǔ méi chī hěn duō fàn　xiàn zài yí dìng è le ba
朋友：你中午没吃很多饭，现在一定饿了吧？

nǐ　shì　yǒu diǎnr è le　yě fēi cháng kě
你：是，有点儿饿了，也非常渴。

péng you　wǒ zhè lǐ yǒu xiāng jiāo hé bǐng gān　nǐ xiǎng chī ma
朋友：我这里有香蕉和饼干，你想吃吗？

nǐ　hǎo　xiè xie
你：好，谢谢。

péng you　wǒ men qù fàn diàn chī hái shì huí jiā zuò fàn
朋友：我们去饭店吃还是回家做饭？

nǐ　zuò fàn tài má fan le　qù fàn diàn ba
你：做饭太麻烦了，去饭店吧。

péng you　nǐ yǐ qián chī guò xī cān méi yǒu
朋友：你以前吃过西餐没有？

nǐ　chī guò hàn bǎo bāo　wǒ xǐ huan chī xiē jiǎn dān de zhōng guó fàn cài
你：吃过汉堡包。我喜欢吃些简单的中国饭菜。

péng you　wǒ men qù chī jiǎo zi　hé chūn juǎn　hǎo ma
朋友：我们去吃饺子和春卷，好吗？

nǐ　hǎo　wǒ ài chī jiǎo zi　kě shì bú huì bāo jiǎo zi
你：好！我爱吃饺子，可是不会包饺子。

Vocabulary

zuò fàn 做饭	to cook	hàn bǎo bāo 汉堡包	burger
fàn 饭	meal; food	rè gǒu 热狗	hot dog
cài shūcài 菜/蔬菜	vegetable	xiā 虾	prawn; shrimp
bái cài 白菜	Chinese leaves	shǔ tiáo 薯条	chips
tǔ dòu 土豆	potato	xiāng jiāo 香蕉	banana
cān tīng 餐厅	canteen	shuǐ guǒ 水果	fruit
zhōng cān 中餐	Chinese meal	píng guǒ 苹果	apple
xī cān 西餐	Western meal	pú táo 葡萄	grape
shí pǐn 食品	food	guǒ zhī 果汁	fruit juice
yǐn liào 饮料	beverage	hǎo chī 好吃	tasty
míng cài 名菜	famous dish	hái shì 还是	or
kǎo yā 烤鸭	roast duck	kě 渴	thirsty
chá guǎn 茶馆	teahouse	è 饿	hungry
miàn miàn tiáo 面/面条	noodles	qǐng 请	to invite; to treat; please
miàn bāo 面包	bread	diǎn cài 点菜	to order dishes
mǐ mǐ fàn 米/米饭	rice; cooked rice	bīng qí lín 冰淇淋	ice-cream
jiǎo zi 饺子	Chinese dumplings	nán nǚ lǎo shào 男女老少	man, woman, old and young; everyone
bāo zi 包子	Chinese buns	má fan 麻烦	trouble
jī jī dàn 鸡/鸡蛋	chicken; egg	jiǎn dān 简单	simple
táng táng guǒ 糖/糖果	sweet	xí guàn 习惯	habit; lifestyle
yú 鱼	fish	yí dìng 一定	must; definitely
hǎi xiān 海鲜	seafood	chūn juǎn 春卷	spring roll
tāng 汤	soup	dú shū 读书	to study; to read
zhū ròu 猪肉	pork	cóng lái 从来	ever
niú ròu 牛肉	beef	bǐng gān 饼干	biscuits
yáng ròu 羊肉	lamb meat; mutton		
niú nǎi 牛奶	milk		

Grammar

1 'verb + 过' is used to describe experiences in the past. When translating into English, 'before' can be added.

- 我学过法文。I have learnt French before.

To make this negative, use '没 + verb + 过' which means 'have/has not … before.'

- 我没学过法文。I have not learnt French before.

2 We have learnt ways of asking questions with 吗, which turn a statement into a question, and with question words such as 哪儿/谁.

哥哥去过中国。 My brother has been to China before.	哥哥去过中国**吗**?	Has your brother been to China before?
	谁去过中国?	Who has been to China before?
	哥哥去过**哪儿**?	Where has your brother been before?

There are many more ways of asking questions.

A You can ask these questions by adding 不 or 没. Use 不 for present tense and 没 for past tense. In the past tense, 了 is left out but 过 stays.

Statement	Present tense question	Past tense question
张校长忙。 Headmaster Zhang is busy	张校长**忙不忙**? Is Headmaster Zhang busy or not?	
李医生是美国人。 Doctor Li is an American.	李医生**是不是**美国人? Is Doctor Li an American or not?	
弟弟有英国地图。 My brother has a map of Britain.	弟弟**有没有**英国地图? Does your brother have a map of Britain or not?	
王护士喜欢看电视。 Nurse Wang likes watching TV.	王护士**喜欢不喜欢**看电视? Does Nurse Wang like watching TV or not?	
中文容易。 Chinese is easy.	中文**容不容易**? Is Chinese easy or not?	
妈妈星期天游泳了。 My mother went for a swim on Sunday.		妈妈星期天**游没游泳**? Did your mother go for a swim on Sunday or not?
我朋友吃过法国饭。 My friend has eaten French cuisine before.		你朋友**吃没吃过**法国饭? Has your friend had French cuisine or not?

B Another way is to add the words 不 (for present tense) or 没有 (for past tense) at the end of a sentence.

- 张老师忙。 ⟶ 张老师忙不？
- 妈妈星期天游泳了。 ⟶ 妈妈星期天游泳了没有？
- 王护士喜欢看电视。 ⟶ 王护士喜欢看电视不？
- 我朋友吃过法国饭。 ⟶ 你朋友吃过法国饭没有？

Tip

是 and 有 structures are not suitable for this type of questioning.

C 吧 is very similar to 吗 in a 'yes or no' question, but with a slight difference in voice. 吧 indicates greater certainty, while 吗 does not. 吧 also has a voice for suggestion, recommendation or persuasion.

Voice	Chinese	English
Not sure	你喜欢吃鸡蛋吗？	Do you like eating eggs?
	你不想去吗？	Don't you want to go?
Sure	你喜欢吃鸡蛋吧？	You like eating eggs, don't you?
	你不想去吧？	You don't want to go, do you?
Suggestive	我们明天去看电影吧！	Let's go and watch a film tomorrow!
	你坐地铁来吧！	Why don't you take the tube?

D You can also add 不/没 in questions ending with 吗/吧. Pay special attention to the answers as they are very different to those in English.

Negative question	You are correct	You are incorrect
你们没有冰淇淋吗？ Don't you have ice-cream?	是的，我们没有冰淇淋。 对，没有。 Correct, we don't have ice-cream. (sounds like: Yes, we don't.)	不是的，我们有冰淇淋。 不对，有。 Incorrect, we do have ice-cream. (sounds like: No, we do.)
这不是牛肉吧？ This isn't beef, is it?	对，这不是牛肉。 Correct, it is not beef.	不对，这是牛肉。 Incorrect, it is beef.

E The structure 'noun/pronoun + 呢？' is very similar to the English structure '… , and you?' or 'What about … ?'.

- 我吃面条，你呢？ I will have the noodles, and you?
- 你们喝果汁，孩子们呢？ You drink juice. What about the children?

Sometimes 呢 can be added to a question sentence to soften the tone of the questioner. 你晚上做什么呢？ sounds more intimate than 你晚上做什么？

F 还是 is used to give alternatives, similar to 'or' in English.

	Chinese	**English**
Adjective	你喜欢热还是冷？	Do you like it hot or cold?
Sentence	贵的好还是便宜的好？	Is the expensive one better or the cheap one?
Verb phrase	你们想看书还是看电视？	Do you want to read books or watch TV?
Noun	你要面条还是米饭？	Do you want noodles or rice?
Noun phrase	妹妹买了大的还是小的？	Did your sister buy the big one or the small one?

Tip

吗 is not needed in these questions.

G When a further confirmation, recommendations or suggestions you can add at the end of a statement phrases like ……吧！……，是吗？……，好吗？, or ……，好不好？

- 你们都吃米饭，是吗？You all have rice, is that right?
- 这里的点心很有名，你要一盘吧！The pastry here is very famous. Why don't you order some (a plateful)!
- 我们不点海鲜，好吗？Shall we not order seafood?
- 今天去饭馆吃晚饭，好不好？Is it all right if we go to a restaurant to have dinner today?

3 The pronouns 这/那 and 这些/那些 can be found after a noun or a list of nouns of the same type.

- 我常常吃羊肉、牛肉这些食品。I often eat lamb, beef, foods like these.
- 他这个人喜欢运动。He (is someone who) likes sports./He, as a person, likes sports.
- 笔、橡皮、尺子这些文具很便宜。Pens, rubbers, rulers, these stationery items are very cheap.

Practice text 11

我叫索菲亚，在英国留学。上个假期我坐飞机回奶奶家，她在马来西亚。我小的时候一直住在奶奶家，养成了多吃水果、蔬菜跟喝汤的习惯。奶奶家后边有果园和菜园：白菜、土豆、苹果树、葡萄藤都有。现在在英国读书了，吃的西餐里有很多羊肉、牛肉这些食品，也常常吃小时候没吃过的汉堡包、薯条和热狗，有点儿不习惯。天天想奶奶做的菜汤、蛋汤和鱼虾汤。吃奶奶做的点心是我们家男女老少的共同爱好！

爸爸妈妈也从新加坡回来了。他们请奶奶去一家西餐厅吃那里的名菜。奶奶从来没吃过西餐。这次吃了以后觉得很好吃，还多点了一份薯条，喝了有牛奶的英国茶。她也喜欢吃这家餐厅的面包和冰淇淋。

1 请阅读课文，然后回答问题。Read the Practice text, and then answer the questions.

- **i** 索菲亚怎么回奶奶家的？
- **ii** 索菲亚小的时候习惯吃什么食品？
- **iii** 现在索菲亚为什么不能常常吃马来食品了？
- **iv** 索菲亚小时候吃过美国外卖吗？
- **v** 索菲亚的爸爸妈妈在哪儿工作？
- **vi** 奶奶喜欢吃西餐厅里的哪两种食品？

2 小文谈她生日时吃的食物和喝的饮料，请看图片。Xiaowen talks about the food and drink she had for her birthday meal. Look at the pictures.
请听录音，选出所提到的食物和饮料。Listen and choose which food and drink is mentioned in the recording.

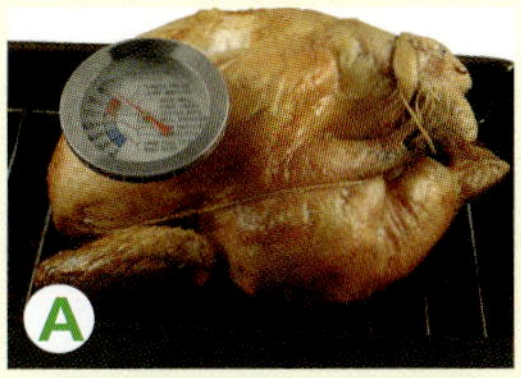

3 请用中文写出你在餐馆里看到的东西。Write in Chinese five things you see in a restaurant.

4 昨天是你的生日。请给你的笔友写一封150字左右的信，信里说：
Yesterday was your birthday. Write a letter of about 150 Chinese characters to your penfriend and say:

- 你吃了什么食品；
- 去了哪儿，跟谁去的；
- 你的朋友都给了你哪些礼物；
- 你晚上做了什么；
- 你的生日好玩儿吗，为什么。

第十二章 健康与健身

Dialogue A

你生病去医院，跟医生说话。You have fallen ill, and are talking to the doctor in the hospital.

yī shēng　nǐ nǎr bù shū fu
医生：你哪儿不舒服？
nǐ　wǒ dù zi zuǐ yá gēn bí zi dōu bù shū fu
你：我肚子、嘴、牙跟鼻子都不舒服。
yī shēng　nǐ shì shén me shí hou shēng de bìng
医生：你是什么时候生的病？
nǐ　zuó tiān zǎo shàng qǐ chuáng de shí hou jiù jiào de bù shū fu
你：昨天早上起床的时候就觉得不舒服。
yī shēng　nǐ qián tiān wǎn shàng chī le xiē shén me
医生：你前天晚上吃了些什么？
nǐ　chī le hěn duō hǎi xiān
你：吃了很多海鲜。
yī shēng　yí dìng shì hǎi xiān bú tài gān jìng nǐ chī guò zhōng yào méi yǒu
医生：一定是海鲜不太干净，你吃过中药没有？
nǐ　méi yǒu wǒ zhǐ chī guò xī yào
你：没有，我只吃过西药。
yī shēng　nǐ jīn tiān jiù zhù yuàn ba yǒu wèn tí ma
医生：你今天就住院吧，有问题吗？
nǐ　méi yǒu kě shì míng tiān jiù chū yuàn
你：没有，可是明天就出院。

Dialogue B

一位医生跟你谈你的身体健康情况。A doctor is discussing your health with you.

yī shēng　zuì jìn nǐ shēn tǐ zěn me yàng
医生：最近你身体怎么样？
nǐ　bǐ yǐ qián chà yǒu shí hou ěr duo yǎn jing gēn shǒu zhǐ dōu téng
你：比以前差，有时候耳朵、眼睛跟手指都疼。
yī shēng　nǐ měi tiān yòng jǐ gè xiǎo shí de diàn nǎo
医生：你每天用几个小时的电脑？
nǐ　xiāng dāng duō wǒ měi tiān yòng shí jǐ gè xiǎo shí de diàn nǎo
你：相当多，我每天用十几个小时的电脑。
yī shēng　nǐ cháng cháng yùn dòng ma
医生：你常常运动吗？
nǐ　bù cháng yùn dòng
你：不常运动。
yī shēng　nǐ dōu zuò xiē shén me tǐ yù huó dòng
医生：你都做些什么体育活动？
nǐ　yǒu shí hou pǎo bù
你：有时候跑步。
yī shēng　nǐ měi tiān jǐ diǎn shuì jiào
医生：你每天几点睡觉？
nǐ　shí èr diǎn zuǒ yòu
你：十二点左右。

Vocabulary

bìng	病	illness
shēng bìng	生病	to fall ill
téng	疼	ache; pain
fā shāo	发烧	to have a fever/ temperature
ké sòu	咳嗽	to cough
gǎn mào	感冒	to catch a cold
dǎ zhēn	打针	injection
chī yào	吃药	to take medicine
yào fáng / yào diàn	药房/药店	pharmacy
cǎo yào	草药	herbal medicine
xī yī / xī yào	西医/西药	Western doctor/ medicine
zhōng yī / zhōng yào	中医/中药	Chinese doctor/ medicine
yī yuàn	医院	hospital
zhù yuàn	住院	to be hospitalized
chū yuàn	出院	to be discharged
shēn tǐ	身体	body; health
kàn bìng	看病	to see a doctor
pàng	胖	fat
shòu	瘦	thin
bǎo	饱	to be full up
ě xīn	恶心	sick; feeling sick
xī yān	吸烟	to smoke
pí jiǔ	啤酒	beer
pú táo jiǔ	葡萄酒	wine
bái jiǔ	白酒	spirits
chéng zhī	橙汁	orange juice
xiū xi	休息	to rest
bǐ / bǐ jiào	比/比较	to compare
zuì	最	most
zuì jìn	最近	recently
qíng kuàng	情况	situation
yào shì … jiù	要是……就	if … then
gòu / zú gòu	够/足够	enough; ample
jiàn kāng	健康	health; healthy
pǎo bù	跑步	running; jogging
bì xū	必须	must; need to
jiāng lái	将来	future
jiāng yào	将要	will
zhòng yào	重要	important
shēng huó	生活	life/to live
bìng rén	病人	patient
jiǎn chá	检查	check up
gào sù	告诉	to tell
xiāng dāng	相当	quite
hǎo chù	好处	benefit; advantage
gēn / hé … yí yàng	跟/和……一样	same as
bù yí yàng	不一样	not the same
tóu	头	head
tóu fa	头发	hair
yǎn jing	眼睛	eyes
bí zi	鼻子	nose
ěr duo	耳朵	ears
yá chǐ	牙齿	teeth
zuǐ ba	嘴巴	mouth
sǎng zi	嗓子	throat
pí fū	皮肤	skin
shǒu	手	hand
shǒu zhǐ	手指	finger
dù zi	肚子	stomach
xīn	心	heart

Grammar

1 As mentioned in Chapters 5 and 6, a sentence ending with 了 can indicate a change of situation, introduce a new situation or talk about something that has just happened or is happening. The same applies to descriptions of illness, medical conditions, general wellbeing and health.

- 爸爸病了，妈妈感冒了，他们都不舒服了。Dad is ill, and Mum has caught a cold. Both are unwell.
- 他好了，他出院了。He got better and was discharged from hospital.

Tip

了 is not used as it is on-going and not a finished action.

2 To explain illness and the location of aches and pains, the word order is: **subject** + **body part** + (**unwell/ache**).

- 张先生眼睛疼。Mr Zhang's eyes hurt/ache.

  To ask questions:
  问：谁眼睛疼？
  问：张先生哪儿疼？
  问：张先生眼睛怎么样？

  to answer:
  答：张先生眼睛疼。

- 昨天小王肚子不舒服。Xiao Wang felt unwell in his stomach yesterday.

  To ask questions:
  问：谁肚子不舒服？
  问：小王什么地方不舒服？
  问：小王肚子怎么样？

  to answer:
  答：小王肚子不舒服。

3 There are generally three ways to make comparisons between two items:

- 比 (to compare) is used to express '… than …'.
- 没有 (not as) is used to express '… is not as … as …'.
- 跟/和……(不)一样 (same/not the same) is used for 'likeness' or 'difference'.

A Remember that the word order is different when making comparisons in Chinese.

Word order in Chinese				Word order in English
Item A	**Structure**	**Item B**	**Adjective**	
中国	比	英国	大	China is larger than Britain.
肉	没有	蔬菜	健康	Meat is not as healthy as vegetables.
红	跟	绿	不一样	Red is not the same as green.

B Comparisons can be made not only between nouns but also between verb phrases and adjectives.

	Chinese	**English**
Verb phrases	坐飞机比坐火车舒服。	Travelling by air is more comfortable than travelling by train.
	吃牛肉没有吃水果健康。	Eating beef is not as healthy as eating fruit.
	在家里学习跟在学校学习一样。	Studying at home is the same as studying at school.
Adjectives	冷比热好。	It is better to be cold than hot.
	远没有近好。	It is better to be close than far away.
	忙跟累不一样。	Being busy is not the same as being tired.

4 The difference between 没有 and 不比 in comparison sentences

- 姐姐不比妹妹高。My elder sister is not taller than my younger sister. (probably the same height)
- 姐姐没有妹妹高。My elder sister is not as tall as my younger sister. (definitely shorter)

5 Some structures may seem like comparison but are not.

- 小花和我有一样的爱好。Xiaohua and I have the same hobbies.
- 小花跟我吃不一样的菜。Xiaohua and I eat different dishes.

In these two sentences, 'Xiaohua and I' is the subject, 'have' and 'eat' are the verbs and 'same hobbies' and 'different dishes' are the objects. They can be turned into comparison sentences:

- 小花的爱好跟我的爱好一样。The hobbies that Xiaohua has are the same as the ones I do.
- 小花吃的菜跟我吃的菜不一样。The dishes Xiaohua eats are not the same as the dishes I eat.

Or simply:

- 小花的爱好跟我的一样。Xiaohua's hobbies are the same as mine.
- 小花的菜跟我的不一样。Xiaohua's dishes are not the same as mine.

Practice text 12

昨天我爸爸感冒了，发烧、咳嗽、嗓子也疼。妈妈跟他一起去医院看病，打了针，下午六点才回来。晚上爸爸吃了一些中草药，在床上休息。

检查爸爸身体的医生告诉妈妈：爸爸的身体不太好，胃有问题。他生病是因为他的生活习惯太差了。

妈妈的生活习惯跟爸爸的很不一样。她不吸烟，吃很多水果、蔬菜，每天都跑步运动。妈妈不胖不瘦，有健康漂亮的长头发和美丽的皮肤。爸爸不比妈妈高，可是比妈妈胖很多。

妈妈跟爸爸说，病人不应该吸烟，也不该喝酒。还说健康最重要，要是他想将来有一个健康的身体，现在开始就必须有一个很好的生活习惯。

1 请阅读课文，然后选择正确的答案。Read the Practice text, and then choose the correct answer to each question.

i 爸爸妈妈什么时候从医院回来？
- A 昨天早上
- B 昨天晚上
- C 昨天下午六点

ii 爸爸生病是因为
- A 他的胃常常疼
- B 他有很不好的生活习惯
- C 他只在星期三吸烟

iii 妈妈吃很多的
- A 肉
- B 水果
- C 烟

iv 妈妈说为了以后的健康
- A 现在就必须不吃肉
- B 应该吃简单的菜
- C 一个人的生活习惯一定要健康

2 朋友们一起谈什么是健康的生活习惯。请看图片。Friends are talking about what healthy lifestyles are. Look at the pictures.
请听录音，选择正确的图片回答问题。Listen to the recording, and choose the correct picture.

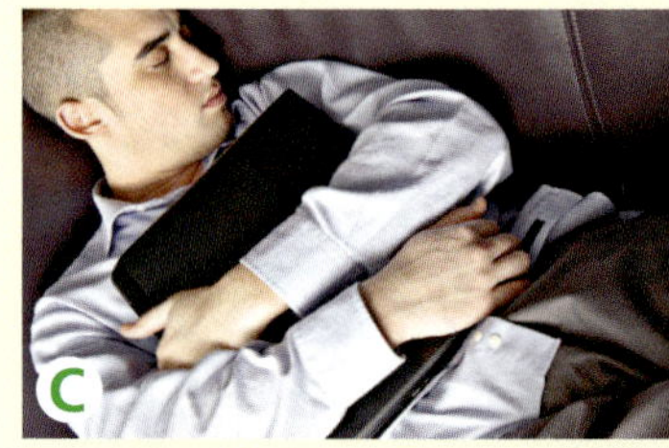

i 红红　**ii** 小林　**iii** 刘英　**iv** 京京　**v** 王美

3 学唱歌。Sing to the tune of *London Bridge is Falling Down* and replace the lyrics with the words in the box below.

London Bridge is Falling Down

A song on examination and illness

fā shāo de shí hou　sǎng zi téng　ěr duo téng　wèi yě téng
发烧的时候，嗓子疼，耳朵疼，胃也疼。
gǎn mào de shí hou　yá chǐ téng　bí zi yě bù shū fu
感冒的时候，牙齿疼，鼻子也不舒服。
kǎo shì de shí hou　yǎn jing téng　dù zi téng　tóu yě téng
考试的时候，眼睛疼，肚子疼，头也疼。
kǎo shì de shí hou　bù chī fàn　bú shuì jiào　bù gāo xìng
考试的时候，不吃饭，不睡觉，不高兴。

4 请用中文写出你在医院里看到的东西。Write in Chinese five things you see in a hospital.

5 扩展练习。Look at the example question and answers below, then write out your own answers to the question given, using the suggestions provided. This exercise can also be used for speaking practice.

	Question	Sample answers
Example:	上个周末你去饭馆吃饭了吗？	• 上个周末我去饭馆吃了中国菜。 • 我跟家人一起去了饭馆。 • 我以前没吃过中国菜，所以很高兴。 • 我觉得中国菜比英国菜好吃。 • 除了烤鸭以外，我还吃了春卷。 • 虽然吃很多肉不健康，可是因为好吃，我吃了很多肉。 • 米饭跟面条一样好吃。 • 妹妹跟我一样，也吃了很多肉。 • 妈妈说在饭馆吃饭有很多好处。 • 她不用做饭，所以很高兴。 • 下个星期天，我想跟朋友一起去饭馆吃饭。
You do it:	你喜欢做饭吗？为什么？	• I like cooking. I learnt to cook when I was little. • I can cook Chinese meals and Western meals. • When cooking, I like to listen to music. • Eating at home has many advantages. • I like to cook with my friends. • I can cook healthy food. • I can also cook food which my family likes to eat. • Cooking is very interesting. • When I am tired, I don't want to cook. • I think food in a restaurant is not as healthy as food at home. • If you eat at a restaurant, you do not need to cook. • Although the food in a restaurant is tasty, they use too much meat.

6 在家吃饭好还是去饭馆吃饭好？《中学杂志》要了解一下学生的看法。请给杂志写一封150字左右的信，信里说：Which is better: eating at home or at a restaurant? *Students Magazine* wants to know students' opinions on this. Write a letter of about 150 Chinese characters to them and say:

- 在家吃饭有哪些好处；
- 在饭馆吃饭有哪些好处；
- 你上次去饭馆都吃了什么饭；
- 要是你有很多钱，你就天天去饭馆吃饭吗，为什么。

Unit test 2

1 反义词。For each word, find its antonym from the box and write it in your exercise book.

旧	放学	热	去	结束	卖	容易	短
少	便宜	小	学	下课	晚	以后	

A 多
B 大
C 买
D 新
E 来
F 贵
G 冷
H 早
I 长
J 难
K 教
L 上学
M 上课
N 以前
O 开始

2 阅读下面的短文。Read the passage.

出国留学

最近二十多年里，相当多的中国家长送孩子去外国上学，英国就有很多的中国学生。来英国学习的好处有很多，除了可以学好英文，英国的住读学校也很有名，教育方法比较好。受到外国的教育对将来上大学或是找工作都会很有用。

抄写下列句子，选择正确的词语填空。Fill in the gap with the correct word from the box. Then copy the sentences in your exercise book.

帮助	英文	比较	多	外语	少	不好	不错

A 中国有不______________家长要孩子去外国上学。
B 要是想学好______________可以去英国留学。
C 英国有教育方法很______________的住读学校。
D 出国留学在找工作上有______________。

3 请给你的中国朋友写一封80–100字的信。信里说：Write your Chinese friend a letter of 80–100 Chinese characters, and say:

- 你最喜欢的老师是谁；
- 他/她教你什么科目；
- 他/她人怎么样，长得什么样；
- 他/她有什么爱好，爱穿什么颜色的衣服；
- 你想要他/她明年还教你吗，为什么。

Did you know ...

gǒu bù lǐ bāo zi
狗不理包子

gǒu bù lǐ bāo zi shì tiān jīn zhù míng de chuán tǒng fēng wèi xiǎo chī yǐ jīng yǒu
狗不理包子是天津著名的传统风味小吃，已经有
yì bǎi wǔ shí duō nián de lì shǐ le
一百五十多年的历史了。

tā de chuàng shǐ rén xìng gāo xiǎo míng wéi gǒu zi tā bú dào èr shí duō suì jiù
它的创始人姓高，小名为狗子。他不到二十多岁就
zhǎng wò le gāo chāo de pēng rèn shǒu yì zài jiā xiāng tiān jīn kāi le yí gè bāo zi pù
掌握了高超的烹饪手艺，在家乡天津开了一个包子铺。
tā zuò de bāo zi bù jǐn wài biǎo měi guā xíng rú jú huā ér qiě xiàn liào xiān xiāng
他做的包子不仅外表美观，形如菊花，而且馅料鲜香，
kǒu gǎn dú tè tā de bāo zi pù hěn kuài yuǎn jìn wén míng shēng yì yuè zuò yuè hǎo
口感独特。他的包子铺很快远近闻名，生意越做越好。

yóu yú gù kè tài duō le gǒu zi zhěng tiān máng de méi yǒu shí jiān gē dà jiā
由于顾客太多了，狗子整天忙得没有时间跟大家
shuō huà lái de rén kàn dào le hù xiāng dǎ qù shuō gǒu zi zhǐ zuò bāo zi
说话。来的人看到了，互相打趣说："狗子只做包子，
bù lǐ rén shí jiān jiǔ le rén men jiù bǎ tā de bāo zi jiào zuò gǒu bù lǐ
不理人。"时间久了，人们就把他的包子叫做"狗不理"。

3 第三单元 国内与国外

Unit 3 The world around us

节日的活动 Activities in festivals

1 What do people eat and do for festivals and special occasions?

A

i

B

ii

C

iii

D

iv

E

v

chūn jié 春节	shēng rì 生日	duān wǔ jié 端午节	shèng dàn jié 圣诞节	yuè bǐng 月饼	lóng zhōu 龙舟
jiǎo zi 饺子	dàn gāo 蛋糕	zhōng qiū jié 中秋节	kàn yuè liang 看月亮	zòng zi 粽子	huǒ jī 火鸡

2 With a partner, discuss traditional festivals that take place in your country and the ways in which they are celebrated.

第十三章 我住的地方

Dialogue A

你在农村的时候，一条蛇咬了你的手。你的邻居跟你谈话。When you were in the countryside, your hand was bitten by a snake. Your neighbour is now talking to you.

lín jū　nǐ shén me dì fāng shòu shāng le
邻居：你什么地方受伤了？
nǐ　wǒ de shǒu shòu shāng le
你：我的手受伤了。
lín jū　shì zuǒ shǒu hái shì yòu shǒu
邻居：是左手还是右手？
nǐ　shì zuǒ shǒu
你：是左手。
lín jū　liú xuě le ma
邻居：流血了吗？
nǐ　hái méi yǒu
你：还没有。
lín jū　shì shé hái shi chóng zi yǎo le nǐ
邻居：是蛇还是虫子咬了你？
nǐ　wǒ xiǎng shì shé
你：我想是蛇。
lín jū　nǐ zhī dào yī yuàn zěn me zǒu ma
邻居：你知道医院怎么走吗？
nǐ　bù zhī dào nǐ kě yǐ gēn wǒ yì qǐ qù ma
你：不知道，你可以跟我一起去吗？

Dialogue B

你跟一位中国朋友谈你的家乡。You are talking about your home town with your Chinese friend.

péng you　nǐ jiā xiāng de fēng jǐng gēn zhèr yí yàng ma
朋友：你家乡的风景跟这儿一样吗？
nǐ　yǒu diǎnr bù tóng nàr de jiào táng bǐ zhèr gāo de duō
你：有点儿不同，那儿的教堂比这儿高得多。
péng you　zuì hǎo wánr de dì fāng shì shén me
朋友：最好玩儿的地方是什么？
nǐ　hǎi tān wǒ xǐ huan yóu yǒng
你：海滩。我喜欢游泳。
péng you　nǐ zài zhōu mò de shí hou zuò xiē shén me
朋友：你在周末的时候做些什么？
nǐ　yǒu shí hou wǒ qù dòng wù yuán qù kàn dà xiàng hóu zi hé měi lì de xiǎo niǎo
你：有时候我去动物园，去看大象、猴子和美丽的小鸟。
péng you　zài nǐ men jiā xiāng kě yǐ mǎi xiē shén me
朋友：在你们家乡可以买些什么？
nǐ　nà er yǒu mài shí pǐn hé yǐn liào de shāng diàn yě yǒu wén jù diàn hé shí zhuāng diàn
你：那儿有卖食品和饮料的商店，也有文具店和时装店。
péng you　nǐ xiǎng huí jiā xiāng shàng dà xué ma
朋友：你想回家乡上大学吗？
nǐ　bù xiǎng wǒ xiǎng qù lún dūn dà xué dú yī kē
你：不想，我想去伦敦大学读医科。

Vocabulary

dì fāng	地方	place
chéng shì / chéng lǐ	城市/城里	city
jiāo qū	郊区	suburb
zhí wù	植物	plant
jiā xiāng	家乡	home town
jiào táng	教堂	church
jū mín	居民	resident
píng fáng	平房	bungalow
bān / bān jiā	搬/搬家	to move house
kōng qì	空气	air
xīn xiān	新鲜	fresh
huán jìng	环境	environment
shā tān	沙滩	beach
hú	湖	lake
shān	山	mountain; hill
shǒu dū	首都	capital (of a country)
tái wān	台湾	Taiwan
cūn zi	村子	village
nóng cūn / xiāng xià	农村/乡下	countryside
dà lóu	大楼	big building
jiàn zhù	建筑	architecture
jiē / jiē dào	街/街道	street
zǒng shì	总是	always
tè bié	特别	special; especially
fù jìn	附近	nearby
huài chù	坏处	disadvantage

ān jìng	安静	quiet
bú dàn … ér qiě	不但……而且	not only ... but also
zǒu	走	to walk; to leave; to get to
qì chē	汽车	car; bus
dǔ chē	堵车	traffic jam
jǐ	挤	to crowd; crowded
jiè shào	介绍	to introduce
bù tóng	不同	not similar (same)
yǔ	与	with; and; to
xiāng jìn	相近	similar
wéi yī	唯一	the only one
gèng	更	even more
yī … jiù	一……就	as soon as ...
gāng / gāng gāng	刚/刚刚	only just
xiàng	像	to look like; to resemble
liú	流	to flow
liú xuě	流血	to bleed
dà xiàng	大象	elephant
niǎo	鸟	bird
hóu zi	猴子	monkey
yā	鸭	duck
lǎo shǔ	老鼠	rat; mouse
shé	蛇	snake
chóng	虫	insect
shòu shāng	受伤	wounded
pà / hài pà	怕/害怕	to fear; afraid

Grammar

1 一点儿 or 得多/多了 can be added to a comparison sentence with 比.

- 姐姐比妹妹高。Elder sister is taller than younger sister.
  姐姐比妹妹高一点儿。Elder sister is a little taller than younger sister.
- 郊区比城里安静。The suburbs are quieter than the city.
  郊区比城里安静多了。The suburbs are a lot quieter than the city.

2 Additional information can also be added to sentences with the structure ……跟/和……一样.

A with adjectives:

- 我的自行车跟小山的自行车一样。My bicycle is the same as Xiaoshan's.
  我的自行车跟小山的自行车一样贵。My bicycle is as expensive as Xiaoshan's.

B with verb phrases:

- 他跟朋友一样。He and his friends are alike.
  他跟朋友一样天天早上去公园跑步。He goes to the park for a run every morning like his friends.

C with a separate sentence:

- 和很多人一样，他不喜欢上班。Like many people, he doesn't enjoy going to work.

3 The structure 像……一样 is similar to 跟……一样 but has the meaning of 'take after someone', 'following the example of …', 'to aspire to …', or 'resemble …'.

- 哥哥像爸爸。My elder brother takes after (resembles) our father.
  哥哥像爸爸一样也想去美国上大学。My elder brother wants to go to study at an American university like our father (following our father's footsteps).

4 Comparative words

A 更/还 (even/even more)
These words generally go before the adjective.

- 这本书比那本书更贵。This book is even more expensive than that one.
- 我哥哥特别高，爸爸比他还高。My brother is very tall and my father is even taller.

B If there is no second item to compare to, you can use 比较喜欢 (to like something more):

- 我比较 喜欢理科科目。I prefer science lessons. (I like them more)
- 老师都比较喜欢暑假。Teachers all prefer the summer holidays. (like summer holidays more than other holidays)

C 更 is used to give preferences, in the phrase 比起……更喜欢…… (similar to 'prefer' in English).

- 比起篮球，我更喜欢足球。I prefer football to basketball.

5 比较 (in comparison/comparatively) and 与……比较 (compared to …)

- 医生说妈妈的生活习惯比较健康。The doctor said that my mother's life style was more (in comparison) healthy.
- 与去年比较，今年的天气更热。Compared to last year, this year is warmer.

6 Superlatives
When you say that something or someone is the tallest, oldest, bravest, smallest and so on, you are using a superlative. In Chinese, 最 (most) is generally placed before an adjective.

- 这本书最好。This book is the best.
- 中秋节的月亮最圆。The moon at Autumn Festival time is the fullest.
- 乡下的空气最新鲜。The air in the countryside is the freshest.

When superlatives are used to give additional information in Chinese, the word order of the sentence is different from English. For example, My neighbour's house is the tallest building in our village.

In English, the superlative 'tallest' is placed before 'in our village', but in Chinese it is the opposite:

我家邻居的房子是**我们村子里**最高的建筑。

More examples:

- 姚明是中国最有名的篮球运动员。Yao Ming is the most famous basketball player in China.

7 最喜欢 (like most)

- 小丽最喜欢在睡觉前看小说。Xiaoli likes to read novels the most before sleeping.
- 奶奶最喜欢去公园散步。Grandma likes to take a stroll in the park the most.

Tip

Adding 的 to 最喜欢 changes the meaning to 'favourite'.

姚明是我最喜欢的运动员。Yao Ming is my favourite sportsman.

Practice text 13

刘丽：

你好！

我昨天刚从家乡回来，今天才回信，请原谅。

我的家乡是农村，在台湾南方。村子左右都是山，后边还有一个湖。山上有植物。这里只有平房，没有大楼。村子里唯一的大街上只有牛车，没有汽车。这个地方不但风景像画儿一样，而且空气也特别新鲜。住在附近的居民喝山上干净的流水，吃湖里的鱼，很少生大病。他们说一觉得不舒服就多喝山水，比医生给的药更有用。

听说你最近刚刚搬家了，郊区的环境一定比城里安静多了吧！街道上也没有城里这么挤吧！你的新房子是什么样的建筑？里边与你的旧房子很相近吗？我跟你一样也总是想离开常常堵车的首都，去比较安静的郊区住。搬去跟你做邻居，怎么样？

祝好！

马云

1 请阅读课文，然后回答问题。Read the Practice text, and write your answers in your exercise book in Chinese.

i 马云刚刚从哪儿回来了？
ii 他家乡有什么样的建筑？
iii 那里的风景怎么样？
iv 住在那个地方的人身体怎么样？
v 他们说什么比吃药更好？
vi 刘丽的新家在什么地方？
vii 马云说城市的街道是什么样的？
viii 首都的交通怎么样？

2 请看下面的图片，找出每人所做的活动。Look at the pictures and find out what activity each person does.

i 红红去湖边散步。
ii 兰兰常常去教堂。
iii 丽丽在动物园看大象。
iv 林林去爬山。

3 请阅读下面的短文。Read the passage.

丽海国家公园

丽海国家公园在中国东部，前边有海，后边有山，风景相当不错，有人说像画儿一样漂亮。这里没有上海那些大城市热闹，因为没有汽车道，但是来这里玩儿的人每年有成千上万。冬天来的人比夏天少，每天不到一千。人们来这里是因为有蓝蓝的天、白白的云和新鲜的空气。

请抄写下列句子，选择正确的词语填空。Copy the sentences below and fill in the gap with the correct word from the box.

漂亮	风景	中间	画儿	几百	一千	空气	安静

i 大海和山的______________是丽海国家公园。

ii 丽海国家公园的______________很美。

iii 因为没有很多汽车，所以比较______________。

iv 冬季每天只有______________人来这里。

4 朋友们在谈住在城市和住在郊区的好处跟坏处。请看图片。Classmates talk about the advantages and disadvantages of living in the city or the countryside. Please look at the pictures

请听录音，选择正确的图片回答问题。Listen, and for each person choose the correct letter.

i 张丽　ii 王林　iii 李文　iv 赵刚　v 马云

5 你刚搬家到了一个新地方。请给笔友写一封150字左右的信，信里说：
You have just moved to a new place. Write your penfriend a letter of about 150 Chinese characters and say:

- 你家附近是什么样的；
- 你周末可以去哪儿玩；
- 那里的环境怎么样；
- 你喜欢住在那儿吗，为什么。

第十四章 问路

Dialogue A

你在某一个中国城市。一个过路人向你问路。You are in a Chinese town. A foreigner who speaks Chinese asks you the way.

lù rén　qǐng wèn　huǒ chē zhàn zài nǎ　yí　gè fāng xiàng
路人：请问！火车站在哪一个方向？
nǐ　zài dōng biān　shùn zhe zhè tiáo mǎ lù　yì zhí wǎng dōng zǒu　zài dì liù gè hóng lǜ dēng de yòu biān
你：在东边，顺着这条马路一直往东走，在第六个红绿灯的右边。
lù rén　yào zǒu duō cháng shí jiān
路人：要走多长时间？
nǐ　zuò chē shí fēn zhōng zuǒ yòu　zǒu lù děi èr shí duō fēn zhōng
你：坐车十分钟左右。走路得二十多分钟。
lù rén　wǒ děi zuò jǐ lù gōng gòng qì chē
路人：我得坐几路公共汽车？
nǐ　wǔ lù　bú yòng huàn chē　qián biān shí zì lù kǒu jiù shì qì chē zhàn
你：五路，不用换车。前边十字路口就是汽车站。
lù rén　wǒ yào děng jǐ fēn zhōng
路人：我要等几分钟？
nǐ　shí fēn zhōng mò bān chē shì wǎn shàng shí yī diǎn bàn
你：十分钟。末班车是晚上十一点半。
lù rén　má fan nǐ le　qǐng wèn chē piào duō shǎo qián
路人：麻烦你了。请问车票多少钱？
nǐ　yí kuài　shì zuì pián yi de jiāo tōng fāng shì
你：一块，是最便宜的交通方式。

Dialogue B

你的一个中国朋友刚来到你住的城市。Your Chinese friend has just arrived in your town.

péng you　zhèr yǒu shén me hǎo wánr de dì fāng
朋友：这儿有什么好玩儿的地方？
nǐ　yǒu bǎi huò gōng sī　tǐ yù chǎng　shì chǎng　shāng chǎng hé miào
你：有百货公司、体育场、市场、商场和庙。
péng you　fù jìn yǒu yóu jú ma　wǒ yào jì xìn hé yóu bāo　mǎi yóu piào hé xìn fēng
朋友：附近有邮局吗？我要寄信和邮包，买邮票和信封。
nǐ　qiáo xià miàn jiù shì yóu jú　xué xiào mén kǒu yě yǒu yóu xiāng
你：桥下面就是邮局，学校门口也有邮箱。
péng you　zuì hǎo de fàn guǎn shì nǎ jiā fàn guǎn
朋友：最好的饭馆是哪家饭馆？
nǐ　xiāng gǎng fàn guǎn　shì wǒ men shěng zuì dà de wài guó fàn guǎn
你：香港饭馆，是我们省最大的外国饭馆。
péng you　dào zhè jiā fàn guǎn zěn me zǒu
朋友：到这家饭馆怎么走？
nǐ　yào huá chuán qù　zài hú duì miàn　páng biān yǒu yí gè yóu lè chǎng
你：要划船去，在湖对面，旁边有一个游乐场。
péng you　cóng zhèr dào hú biān yào zǒu jǐ fēn zhōng
朋友：从这儿到湖边要走几分钟？
nǐ　zhǐ yào wǔ fēn zhōng　lí xué xiào hěn jìn
你：只要五分钟，离学校很近。

Vocabulary

hóng lǜ dēng 红绿灯	traffic lights
jìn kǒu rù kǒu 进口/入口	entrance
lù kǒu 路口	road junction
lù 路	bus number; route
lù mǎ lù 路/马路	road
shí zì lù kǒu 十字路口	crossroad
guò lù rén 过路人	passer-by
lù guò 路过	to go past
fāng xiàng 方向	direction
xiàng wǎng 向/往	towards
guǎi zhuǎn 拐/转	to turn
shùn zhe 顺着	to follow; along
lí 离	(distance) from
jìn 近	near; close
yuǎn 远	far
gōng lǐ 公里	kilometre
shěng 省	province
dì zhǐ zhù zhǐ 地址/住址	address
dān yuán 单元	unit
bǎi huò shāng diàn 百货商店	department store
gōng chǎng 工厂	factory
shì chǎng 市场	market
yín háng 银行	bank
yóu jú 邮局	post office
huàn 换	to change
piào 票	ticket
zhěn suǒ 诊所	clinic
miào 庙	temple
qiáo 桥	bridge
tǐ yù chǎng 体育场	sports ground
dì diǎn 地点	location; place
fēi jī chǎng 飞机场	airport
qì chē zhàn 汽车站	bus station
děi 得	to need to; should
kuài 快	fast; quick
biàn huà 变化	change
hòu lái 后来	later (on)
yǒu kòng yǒu kòngr 有空/有空儿	free time
chū chū lái 出/出来	out; to come out from/of
chū zū qì chē 出租汽车	taxi
mén kǒu dà mén 门口/大门	door; gate
jì 寄	to mail; to send
yóu piào 邮票	stamp
yóu bāo 邮包	parcel
xìn xiāng 信箱	letter box
xìn fēng 信封	envelope
bān 班	bus number
mò bān chē 末班车	last service (bus)
děng 等	to wait
yóu lè chǎng 游乐场	amusement park
shāng chéng 商城	shopping mall
shāng chǎng 商场	market
mí lù 迷路	to become lost
xiǎo chī diàn 小吃店	snack bar
shì 事	thing; matter
bāo 包	to wrap up
bù fen 部分	part; section

Grammar

1 问路 (asking for directions) and 指路 (giving directions)

A There are at least three different ways of asking for directions. The word order is:

(place) + 在哪儿？ Where is (place)?

(place) + 在哪个方向？ (place) is in which direction?

去 + (place) + 怎么走？ How do I get to (place)?

- 请问！银行在哪儿？ Excuse me! Where is the bank?
- 请问！邮局在哪个方向？ Please may I ask, which direction is the post office in?
- 请问！去火车站怎么走？ Excuse me! How do I get to the train station?

B There are many ways of giving directions.

a The simplest way is to use 在 + direction/position word.

- 银行在前边。The bank is ahead (in front).
- 邮局在东边。The post office is in the east (to your east side).
- 火车站在邮局后边。The train station is behind the bank.

b To give more detailed directions, you must place the location or direction before the verbs 'to turn' and 'to go'. The word order is:

顺着 + place + 走 (follow …)

往/向 + direction + 走/拐/转 (go/turn to …)

- 顺着马路走。Follow the road and proceed.
- 顺着马路往前走。Follow the road and walk straight ahead.
- 在十字路向右拐。Turn right at the crossroads.

c To give information on distance, the word order is: 离 + place + far/near/length of time or distance.

- 商场离这儿很近，五分钟就到。The market is quite close, five minutes from here.
- 游乐场离学校很远，有二十多公里。The amusement park is very far from the school, more than twenty kilometres away.

d You can suggest the means of transport with 可以 or duration with 得 or 要.

- 你可以坐八路公共汽车去，很方便。You can take the number eight bus, very convenient.
- 走路去得十五分钟左右。It will take around fifteen minutes to get there on foot.

Tip
得 is a verb in this context, meaning 'to need/require'.

2 Description of movement 'to and from'

The word order is:

从 + place + 来 (coming from a place)

到 + place + 去 (heading to a place).

- 他从上海来。He comes from Shanghai.
- 今天我们一家人要到饭馆去吃晚饭。Today our whole family will go to a restaurant for our evening meal.

A Both '去 + a place' and '到 + a place + 去' mean 'to go to a place'.

- 玛丽要去中国。Mary wants to go to China. (She wants to.)
- 玛丽要到中国去。Mary wants/needs to go to China. (There is a need.)

B 到 is used to mean 'to reach, to arrive', and it can be used with another verb to show that an action has been fully completed or achieved. For example:

走	to walk/go	走到	to get to/arrive
看	to look/read	看到	to see/saw
学	to learn	学到	to learn and obtain/master
买	to buy	买到	to have bought/manage to buy
寄	to post	寄到	to post to
来	to come	来到	to arrive

- 走到百货商店，往左转。When you reach the department store, turn left.
- 我在美国买到了米老鼠玩具。In the USA I managed to buy a Mickey Mouse toy.
- 邮包寄到哪儿？寄到上海。Where was the parcel posted to? Shanghai.
- 我是两个星期前来到这里的。I arrived here two weeks ago.

3 When an action only takes place for a short period of time, verbs in Chinese are often duplicated (repeated).

- 我想看书。I want to read books.
  我想看看书。I want to have a look at books.
- 妈妈去公园散步。Mother goes to walk in the park.
  妈妈去公园散散步。Mother goes to the park for a (short) walk.

Sometimes the duplicated verbs are separated by 一.

- 这本书怎么样？我看一看可以吗？How is this book? Can I have a look?
- 我不知道这两条鱼哪一个好，我们比一比吧！I don't know which of these two fish is better. Let's have a go at comparing them.

You can also add 一下, 一会儿 or (一)点儿 to a verb.

- 我总是先看一会儿书，然后才睡觉。I always read for a little while first before going to sleep.
- 我不想睡觉，我想看点儿书。I don't want to sleep; I want to read a little.
- 你饿了吧？先吃一点儿蛋糕，我们一会儿到饭馆去吃饭。You must be hungry. Have some cake first. We will head to the restaurant for our meal shortly.

4 Summary of 的, 地, 得 structures

The key to understanding and using these three words properly is to be very clear about their position in a sentence.

A 的 is for describing nouns, so it is always placed before nouns.

美丽的花 beautiful flowers
我的笔 my pens
妈妈做的鱼 the fish that Mum cooked
从英国来的信 letter from the UK

B 地 is for describing verbs, explaining how the action is being carried out, such as 'speak slowly' or 'read carefully'. It always goes before a verb.

- 你应该慢慢地吃饭。You should eat slowly.
- 学生们都认真地学习。Students all study diligently.
- 大家都努力地工作。Everyone is working hard.

In everyday language, the structure is much more casual, especially in commands/instructions.

- 快走！ Walk fast! (omitting two characters)
- 慢点儿写！ Write a little more slowly! (replace 地 with 点儿)
- 好好吃！ Eat your food properly!

Tips

- Adjectives can be turned into adverbs by adding 地.
- The adjective before 地 needs to be two or more characters.
- Single character adjectives need to be repeated, such as 慢慢地.
- 地 can sometimes be omitted.
  你应该慢慢吃饭。
  学生们都认真学习。
  大家都努力工作。

C 得 is used for describing verbs, explaining what progress has been achieved, or not. It is preceded by a verb and followed by an adjective, phrase or even a sentence.

- 奶奶走得慢。Grandma walks slowly.
- 昨天我睡得不太好。Yesterday I slept badly.
- 那个孩子玩儿得忘了写作业。He enjoyed playing so much that he forgot to write his homework.
- 那个孩子玩儿得饭也不吃了。He played and played, and even neglected his meals.

For sentences with an object, 得 cannot simply be placed between the verb and the object, nor behind the object. For this reason, the verb of the sentence needs to be repeated. Word order:

Subject + verb + object + (repeated) verb + 得 + adjective

- 哥哥打篮球打得好。My brother plays basketball well.
- 我说德文说得不流利。I don't speak German fluently.

Sometimes, the first verb can be left out.

- 哥哥篮球打得好。
- 我德文说得不流利。

To express 'one person does something better than another person', there are different ways to insert the 比 structure.

	With repeated verb	**Without repeated verb**
He learns Chinese well.	他学中文学得好。	他中文学得好。
He learns Chinese better than me.	他**比我**学中文学得好。 他学中文**比我**学得好。 他学中文学得**比我**好。	他**比我**中文学得好。 他中文**比我**学得好。 他中文学得**比我**好。

Practice text 14

家乡的变化（一）

我叫林小友。从前我住的城市与现在有很大的不同。那时候路上差不多都是骑自行车的人，汽车很少。从我家到我读小学的学校去不用很长时间。因为很近，所以我也骑自行车上学。每天早早地从家里出来，顺着马路很快地骑到十字路口，然后往左拐，先路过一个玩具工厂，然后是儿童诊所。离诊所一百米的地方是银行，银行旁边有一个公园，公园后边就是我的学校。那时候我认识城里的每一条街道和每一个大楼。每天骑车走三公里的路，不但做了运动，而且也看了风景，车也骑得特别快。

1 请阅读课文，然后选择唯一正确的答案。Read the Practice text, and then answer each question by choosing the only correct answer.

i 林小友从前住的城市是什么样的？
- **A** 路上没有很多汽车。
- **B** 路上差不多都是汽车。
- **C** 与现在没有不同。

ii 林小友的小学学校在哪儿？
- **A** 从他家去要用很长时间。
- **B** 离他家不远。
- **C** 不能骑自行车去。

iii 儿童诊所在哪儿？
- **A** 学校和公园中间。
- **B** 他家后边。
- **C** 玩具工厂和银行中间。

iv 林小友喜欢骑自行车，因为
- **A** 可以看到朋友
- **B** 可以慢慢骑
- **C** 很健康

2 小赵到广州去玩儿，跟导游聊天。请看图片。Xiao Zhao is travelling in Guangzhou. He chats with the tour guide. Look at the pictures. 请听下面的对话，找出五个小赵在广州要去的地方。Listen, and choose five places Xiao Zhao will go while in Guangzhou.

3 你刚到你朋友的家度假，她向你介绍附近有些什么地方。请看图片。You have arrived at your friend's house to spend the holiday there. She is telling you about the location of a few places near her home. Look at the pictures.

请听录音，将图片的字母分别填入适当的方格内。Listen and put the correct letter in the appropriate box.

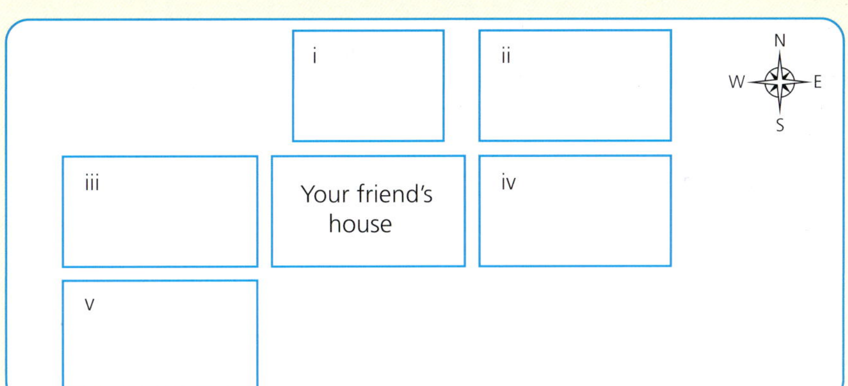

4 讲个故事吧! Story time! Learn the story below and try to tell it to your friends, or alternatively write your own story using the vocabulary provided in the box.

小明的故事 Story by Xiaoming	有一天，我跟朋友大山来到市中心的公园玩球。那里的风景很漂亮，人也不多。我们看到一个中国老人在湖边打太极拳。他的太极拳比我们的体育老师好。我们就不玩球了，在老人旁边看他的太极拳。老人看到我们，不打了，跟我们说："你们想学太极拳吗？"我们高兴地说："想！" 我们一起跟老人学太极拳。老人是从中国来的，他人很友好，英语也说得不错。大山的体育从小就很好，也很聪明。他太极拳打得比我好。后来我们去商店买到了一个大蛋糕，跟老人一起吃。那一天很开心。
你的故事 Your story	有一天 one day 跟……说 say (said) to … 那一天 that day 后来 later on

5 你和朋友在公园里踢足球，一个你们不认识的人走过来跟你们说话。请写150字左右，说说：You and your friends are playing football and a stranger comes and talks to you. Write about 150 Chinese characters and say:

- 他/她为什么要跟你们说话；
- 你觉得应该怎么做；
- 你们都说了些什么；
- 后来发生了什么事。

6 请将下列段落翻译成英文。Translate the following paragraph into English.

家乡的变化 (二)

后来我到伦敦去上大学，每次回家，都会看到更多的新楼、高楼，街上的出租车也一年比一年多了。后来爸爸妈妈搬家住进了一座很高的大楼里。以前我朋友的地址都有路名和街名，现在变了，跟我家一样都是楼号和单元号了。有一天，我有空儿，没有太多事，想到以前常常路过的公园去看一看。骑车走到十字路口就迷路了。附近的环境变化得太大了！有很多我不认识的新街道。以前玩具厂的地点现在是地铁站和小吃店，从那里可以坐地铁去飞机场。我不能骑自行车从地铁站到学校去，因为中间已经没有自行车道了。

第十五章 业余时间

Dialogue A

你在一家百货商店给妈妈买衣服。跟那里的售货员说话。You are in a department store buying clothes for your mother, and are talking to the assistant there.

shòu huò yuán　huān yíng guāng lín　nǐ xiǎng gěi nǐ de mā ma mǎi shén me yī fu
售货员：欢迎光临！你想给你的妈妈买什么衣服？
nǐ　mào zi　wéi jīn　qún zi huò zhě shǒu tào　wà zi　xiān kàn kan máo yī
你：帽子、围巾、裙子或者手套、袜子。先看看毛衣。
shòu huò yuán　nǐ yào shén me yán sè de
售货员：你要什么颜色的？
nǐ　hóng sè gēn hēi sè de
你：红色跟黑色的。
shòu huò yuán　zhè jiàn kě yǐ ma　dà xiǎo hé shì ma
售货员：这件可以吗？大小合适吗？
nǐ　dà xiǎo hěn hé shì　jià gé yě hé shì　wǒ yào zhè jiàn　wǒ hái xiǎng mǎi chèn yī
你：大小很合适，价格也合适，我要这件。我还想买衬衣。
shòu huò yuán　nǐ xiǎng mǎi jǐ jiàn
售货员：你想买几件？
nǐ　liǎng jiàn　hái xiǎng kàn kan duǎn kù
你：两件。还想看看短裤。
shòu huò yuán　tā xiàng nǐ yí yàng gāo ma
售货员：她像你一样高吗？
nǐ　chà bù duō yí yàng
你：差不多一样。

Dialogue B

你去银行换钱，跟那里的工作人员说话。You are in a bank changing money, and are talking to the assistant there.

gōng zuò rén yuán　nǐ xiǎng huàn duō shǎo qián
工作人员：你想换多少钱？
nǐ　yì qiān wǔ bǎi kuài　shāng diàn dà jiǎn jià　wǒ yào mǎi hěn duō yī fu
你：一千五百块。商店大减价，我要买很多衣服。
gōng zuò rén yuán　nǐ xiǎng qù nǎ gè yī fu diàn
工作人员：你想去哪个衣服店？
nǐ　shāng chéng lǐ de bǎi huò shāng diàn　nà lǐ de yī fu dōu dǎ wǔ zhé
你：商城里的百货商店，那里的衣服都打五折。
gōng zuò rén yuán　nà lǐ de gù kè duō ma
工作人员：那里的顾客多吗？
nǐ　hěn duō　yīn wèi dà duō shù de dōng xi dōu dǎ zhé　hěn pián yi
你：很多，因为大多数的东西都打折，很便宜。
gōng zuò rén yuán　nǐ hái zhǔn bèi mǎi bié de dōng xi ma
工作人员：你还准备买别的东西吗？
nǐ　wǒ hái xiǎng kàn kan shǒu jī hé xiǎo shōu yīn jī
你：我还想看看手机和小收音机。
gōng zuò rén yuán　nǐ hé shuí yì qǐ qù
工作人员：你和谁一起去？
nǐ　wǒ de tóng xué　tā men dōu xiǎng mǎi xīn shì de píng guǒ shǒu jī
你：我的同学，他们都想买新式的苹果手机。

Vocabulary

yán sè	颜色	colour
bái	白	white
hēi	黑	black
huáng	黄	yellow
hóng	红	red
lán	蓝	blue
lǜ	绿	green
yín sè	银色	silver
jīn sè	金色	gold
chéng sè	橙色	orange
huī sè	灰色	grey
kā fēi sè	咖啡色	brown
dài	带	to take; to bring; to carry
yǎng	养	to raise; to keep
guàng	逛	to stroll; to wander
wánr	玩儿	to have fun; to play
yán sè sè	颜色/色	colour
xié	鞋	shoe
yùn dòng xié	运动鞋	trainers; sneakers
wéi jīn	围巾	scarf
shǒu tào	手套	glove
kù zi	裤子	trousers
niú zǎi kù	牛仔裤	jeans
duǎn kù	短裤	shorts
mào zi	帽子	hat/cap
wà zi	袜子	sock
qún zi	裙子	skirt
yī fu	衣服	clothes
máo yī	毛衣	jumper; sweater
chèn yī	衬衣	underclothes; shirt
chèn shān	衬衫	blouse; shirt
dà yī	大衣	coat
shàng yī	上衣	top
yǔ yī	雨衣	raincoat
dǎ zhé	打折	discount
jiǎn jià	减价	reduced price
jià qián jià gé	价钱/价格	price
zhǎo qián	找钱	(to give) change
cì biàn	次/遍	number of times
yǒu de	有的	some
bié de	别的	other; else
jì xù	继续	to continue
yě cān	野餐	picnic
zhǐ hǎo	只好	can only
lìng lìng wài	另/另外	another; also
yòu	又	and; again
zài	再	(future) once more
gù kè	顾客	customer
huān yíng guāng lín	欢迎光临	welcome
shǒu jī	手机	mobile phone
shōu yīn jī	收音机	radio
yóu xì jī	游戏机	game console
huài	坏	broken; bad; worn
dà xiǎo	大小	size
hé shì	合适	reasonable; suitable
lèi	累	tired
wán wán chéng	完/完成	to complete
chuān dài	穿/戴	to wear
céng	层	layer; floor
màn	慢	slow
suī rán kě shì dàn shì	虽然……可是/但是	although; but
yì biān yì biān	一边……一边……	do two things at the same time
dà duō shù	大多数	majority

Grammar

1 就 and 才

These two words are adverbs. They have no fixed meaning but they change the tone of the sentence. They are placed before verbs, adjectives or other adverbs.

A 就 is similar to the English phrases 'as early as' or 'already'. 才 is similar to 'until'.

- 我从小就开始学英文了。I began to learn English when I was little.
- 我朋友中学才开始学英文。My friend did not begin to learn English until she/he was in secondary school.
- 我们到伦敦的第一天就去了伦敦大桥。The first day we arrived in London, we immediately went to London Bridge.

B 就 is used for quick actions. 才 is used for actions that happen only when certain conditions are met.

- 那个孩子一看见熊猫就笑了。The child smiled as soon as he/she saw the giant panda.
- 我来伦敦以后才知道英国没有很多晴天。I did not realize until I arrived in London that there are not many sunny days in Britain.

C 就 is used when something mentioned earlier is true. 才 is used to contradict something that was mentioned earlier.

- 他就是我早上跟你说的那个德文老师。He is none other than the German teacher I talked to you about this morning.
- 这就是我去年认识的美国朋友。This is none other than the American friend I became acquainted with last year.
- 这才是我要买的书。Now this is the book I have wanted to buy!

D 就 is used when something will happen very soon. 才 is used when something will take a while.

- 前边左拐就到学校了。Turn left up ahead and you will be at the school.
- 一个小时以后才能到学校。It will take at least an hour to get to school.

E 就 and 才 change the tone of the speaker.

- 他三点就来了。He came at three o'clock. (He came as early as three – that early!)
- 他三点才来。He came at three o'clock. (He did not arrive until three o'clock – that late!)

2 You can use 遍 to talk about how many times an action takes place. For example:

- 他看这个美国电影。He watches this American film.
  这个美国电影他看了三遍。He watched this film three times.

次 and 遍 both tell us how often an action occurs, but 遍 emphsizes on completing the entire process of the action.

- 那本小说我看了两遍。I read that novel twice.
- 他的歌我每天可以听一百遍。I can listen to his songs a hundred times every day.

Tip

Notice how the word order was changed; the object is moved to the start of the sentence.

3 In English, verbs have different tenses. Chinese verbs, however, are different. They need a second verb, an adjective or 了 to tell the tense.

A Infinitive verb + 完:

- 吃 to eat —— 吃完 to finish eating
- 看 to read ——看完 to finish reading
- 做 to do ——做完 to finish (doing)

Tip

The use of 了 has been discussed in Chapter 5.

B Infinitive verb + 到:

- 买 to buy —— 买到 bought
- 看 to look —— 看到 to see/saw
- 听 to listen ——听到 to hear/heard

C Infinitive verb + 回:

- 找 to look for/to give change —— 找回 to find/to receive change
- 走 to walk —— 走回 to walk back

D Infinitive verb + adjective:

- 走 to walk —— 走累 tired from walking
- 戴 to put on —— 戴好/戴坏 have worn properly/have worn through
- 写 to write —— 写对/写错 have written correctly/wrongly
- 变 to change —— 变好/变坏 change for the better/worse
- 穿 to wear —— 穿上/穿好/穿坏 to put on/have worn properly/have worn through

Practice text 15

去香港

我叫琳达。今年暑假爸爸妈妈带我去香港玩儿了三天。香港的地铁很方便，我们每天都坐三、四次。香港有一个海洋公园，那里养了很多水生动物，每天来的人很多，有的还在那里野餐。

我最喜欢的活动是逛街。我买了运动鞋和牛仔裤。妈妈给爸爸买了新帽子，因为他的旧帽子已经戴坏了。香港的东西太便宜了！我们买了很多衣服，还找回了一些钱。

除了买东西以外，我们还去看了两个电影，一个是英国电影，另外一个是香港电影。香港电影相当有趣，我们第二天吃完了晚饭又去看了一遍。

香港的夏天虽然不冷，但是常常下雨。有一次我们刚离开商店，天就下雨了！我们只好回去又买了雨衣穿上，继续逛街。

明年我还要再去一次。

1 请阅读课文，然后回答问题。Read the Practice text and write the answers to the questions in Chinese in your exercise book.

i 琳达和家人在香港玩了多久？
ii 他们常用什么交通方式？
iii 除了看水生动物以外，人们还去海洋公园做什么？
iv 琳达在香港喜欢做什么？(给出两个例子。)
v 妈妈为什么给爸爸买帽子？
vi 那个香港电影他们看了几遍？
vii 琳达明年旅游有什么打算？

2 请阅读下面的短文。Read the passage.

> **便利的打折店**
>
> 我们家乡从前没有打折店，今年刚开了一家，就在市中心，是这里唯一的打折店。店里不但有日常用品，而且也有文具和食品。交通也很方便，从火车站坐公共汽车去只需要十分钟。从我家顺着马路骑自行车五分钟就到。我跟朋友每个星期都去买两次东西。

请抄写下列句子，选择正确的词语填空。Copy the sentences below and fill in the gap with the correct word from the box.

别的	第一个	一次	两次
近	五分钟	又	十分钟

i 除了今年开的店，家乡没有____________打折店。
ii 人们又可以买文具____________可以买吃的东西。
iii 我家离打折店比较____________。
iv 我每三、四天去____________打折店。

3 你在百货商店买东西，在那里工作的售货员给你介绍。请看图片。You are shopping in a department store. The shop assistant is telling you about the store. Please look at the pictures.
请听录音，选择正确答案。Listen, and choose the correct picture.

4 请用中文写出你在百货商店看到了什么。Write in Chinese five things you see in a department store.

5 你考试成绩很不错，周六妈妈带你去逛街。请写一篇150字左右的文章，内容包括：You did well in the exam. Your mother took you shopping on Saturday. Write an essay of about 150 Chinese characters including the following:

- 那天的天气怎么样；
- 你们去了哪些地方；
- 你们买了什么东西；
- 你觉得这个周末怎么样。

第十六章 保护环境

Dialogue A

你刚从山区回来，和你的一个中国朋友谈话。You have just returned from the mountain region, and are talking to a Chinese friend.

péng you　nǐ gāng gāng qù guò de nà gè dì qū jìn kuàng zěn me yàng
朋友：你刚刚去过的那个地区近况怎么样？
nǐ　nà lǐ de sēn lín pò huài hěn yán zhòng
你：那里的森林破坏很严重。
péng you　nǐ dōu qù le nǎ xiē dì fāng
朋友：你都去了哪些地方？
nǐ　shān qū hé hú qū　nà lǐ de shù lín bǐ shí nián qián shǎo le
你：山区和湖区。那里的树林比十年前少了。
péng you　yě shēng dòng wù de shēng huó tiáo jiàn zěn me yàng
朋友：野生动物的生活条件怎么样？
nǐ　zhí wù shǎo le　dòng wù měi tiān dōu yǒu è dù zi de wēi xiǎn
你：植物少了，动物每天都有饿肚子的危险。
péng you　nàr de qì hòu zěn me yàng
朋友：那儿的气候怎么样？
nǐ　qì hòu hái kě yǐ　xià tiān yǒu zú gòu de yáng guāng
你：气候还可以，夏天有足够的阳光。
péng you　nǐ zài nàr dōu zuò le xiē shén me
朋友：你在那儿都做了些什么？
nǐ　wǒ cān jiā le yí gè jiù hù yě shēng dòng wù de huó dòng
你：我参加了一个救护野生动物的活动。

Dialogue B

你在海边一家茶馆，跟一位老师谈环境问题。You are at a tea house by the seaside, chatting to a teacher about environmental problems.

lǎo shī　nǐ cháng cháng lái hǎi biān wánr ma
老师：你常常来海边玩儿吗？
nǐ　yǐ qián bù cháng lái　rén men luàn diū dōng xi　hěn zāng　xiàn zài hǎo duō le
你：以前不常来，人们乱丢东西，很脏。现在好多了。
lǎo shī　shì zěn me biàn hǎo de
老师：是怎么变好的？
nǐ　jǐng chá tiān tiān lái yán jìn dà jiā luàn diū dōng xi
你：警察天天来严禁大家乱丢东西。
lǎo shī　nǐ jué de zài huán jìng wèn tí shàng　zuì yào jǐn de shì shén me
老师：你觉得在环境问题上，最要紧的是什么？
nǐ　bì xū zài rì cháng shēng huó zhōng nǔ lì　lì rú shǎo yòng shuǐ diàn
你：必须在日常生活中努力，例如少用水电。
lǎo shī　nǐ zài bǎo hù huán jìng fāng miàn dōu zuò xiē shén me
老师：你在保护环境方面都做些什么？
nǐ　wǒ gēn péng you zhǔn bèi xīng qī tiān qù hé biān zhòng shù
你：我跟朋友准备星期天去河边种树。
lǎo shī　wǒ kě yǐ gēn nǐ men yì qǐ qù ma
老师：我可以跟你们一起去吗？
nǐ　hǎo a　huān yíng nín lái gēn wǒ men yì qǐ zhòng shù
你：好啊！欢迎您来跟我们一起种树！

Vocabulary

dì qū	地区	region
shān qū	山区	mountain region
hǎi hǎi biān	海/海边	sea; seaside
hé	河	river
shù lín	树林	woods
sēn lín	森林	forest
rén kǒu	人口	population
yě shēng	野生	wild
tài yáng	太阳	sun
yáng guāng	阳光	sunshine
qì hòu	气候	climate
zhǐ yǒu … cái	只有……才	only if … then
fāng miàn	方面	side; aspect
bǎo hù	保护	to protect
yuán yīn	原因	reason
gēn jù	根据	based on
pò huài	破坏	to devastate
yán zhòng	严重	serious
duì	对	to
wèi	为	for
xiàng … xué xí	向……学习	to learn from
zhòng	种	to plant
xuǎn zé	选择	to choose; to select
zhǎng zhǎng de	长/长得	to grow
jìn zhǐ yán jìn	禁止/严禁	to forbid
wēi xiǎn	危险	danger

zāng	脏	dirty
lì hài	厉害	to a serious degree
kuài lè	快乐	happy
nán guò	难过	sad
kě xī	可惜	pity
luàn	乱	chaotic/untidy
guān xi	关系	to relate/relationship
jī huì	机会	opportunity
lì rú bǐ rú	例如/比如	for example
yóu yú	由于	due to
jiù jiù hù	救/救护	to save
jǐng chá jú	警察(局)	police (station)
hái kě yǐ	还可以	OK
diū	丢	to throw away/lose
jīng guò	经过	with/by
dà jiā	大家	everyone
guān yú	关于	regarding
shì	试	to try
yào jǐn	要紧	essential
sǐ	死	to die
zhào gù	照顾	to look after
zhí yuán	职员	staff member
xìng gé	性格	personality
tè diǎn	特点	characteristic
dà zì rán	(大)自然	nature

Grammar

1 The verb 在 can follow a main verb to give the location of the action.

- 小明住在中国，他朋友玛丽住在伦敦。Xiaoming lives in China. His friend Mary lives in London.
- 弟弟坐在床上，小猫睡在沙发上。My brother is sitting on the bed. The kitten is sleeping on the sofa.

Tip

Notice that it is different in these sentences.

- We eat lunch at school.
  我们吃中餐在学校。✘
  我们在学校吃中餐。✔

2 More on time expressions

A time/action + (的)时候

- 小(的)时候 when young
- 上五年级的时候 during the fifth grade
- 上课的时候 while having lessons

B time/action + 以前

- 三年(以)前 three years ago
- 吃晚饭以前 before having the evening meal

C time/action + 以后

- 两年以后 two years later
- 起床以后 after getting up

- 爸爸十五岁的时候去了英国。My father went to the UK at the age of fifteen.
- 吃饭的时候不应该说太多。During meal times, you should not talk too much.
- 十年前我住在法国。Ten years ago I lived in France.

3 The phrase 从……到…… (from … to …) can be used to refer to distance in space as well as in time.

- 从北京到上海　从商店到公园　从美国到英国　从我家到学校
- 从冬天到夏天　从五岁到十岁　从星期一到星期六　从早到晚
- 老师从北京到伦敦去。The teacher will go to London from Beijing.
- 从我家到学校走路得十五分钟。It takes fifteen minutes to get to school from my home on foot.
- 从星期一到星期六我每天都有课。I have lessons every day from Monday till Saturday.

4 'It' in English can represent almost anything: the weather, seasons, objects, time, distance, phrases and even long sentences.

- It is **cold** today.
- It is very important **to protect the environment**.
- It takes eleven hours **to go to China from the UK by air**.
- It takes twenty minutes **for us to walk back home from the train station**.
- It is truly wonderful **to be able to work with you**.
- It is beneficial to our health **to eat lots of vegetables**.

In Chinese, however, it is not possible to use 它 in the same way.

- 今天天气冷。
- 保护环境很重要。
- 从中国坐飞机去英国要十一个小时。
- 我们从火车站走路回家得二十分钟。
- 能跟你们在一起工作真是太快乐了！
- 吃很多蔬菜对我们的身体健康有好处。

5 Prepositions such as to, for, at, and from in English take the structure 对/为/向 + noun/pronoun in Chinese. This structure should always be placed before the verb in sentences.

A 对 (to, for, at)

- 爷爷给孙女一个苹果，孙女对爷爷笑了。Grandpa gave his granddaughter an apple. She smiled at him.
- 多问问题对学习有帮助。It helps your studies to ask lots of questions.

B 为 (for, for sake of)

- 爸爸为一家人的生活从早到晚地工作。My father works day and night for the upkeeping of the whole family.

C 向 (from, to)

- 丽丽很努力，我应该向她学习。Lily is very hard-working. I should learn from her.
- 回家的时候请向你父母问好。When you go home, please pass on my greetings to your parents.

6 经过 + noun/noun phrase means 'through the process of, with or by'.

- 经过努力，我的英文水平提高了很多。Through hard work, my English has improved a great deal.
- 经过医生们每时每刻的照顾，奶奶的身体好多了。With round-the-clock care from the doctors, grandma's health has improved a lot.

7 也 (also) / 还 (in addition) / 又 (again) / 再 (once more)

A Either 也 or 还 can be used for sentences with one subject.
小明买了蔬菜，也买了水果。/ 小明买了蔬菜，还买了水果。
Xiaoming bought vegetables and also fruit. ('Xiaoming' is the only subject.)

B 还 cannot be used for sentences with more than one subjects, so use 也 for these.
中国人喜欢熊猫，外国人也喜欢熊猫。
Chinese people like giant pandas, and so do foreigners. (The subjects are 'Chinese people' and 'foreigners'.)

C 又 is for something reoccurring, regular and expected:

- 又下雨了！ It is raining again!

D 再 is normally for future tense or the expression 'ever since' or 'never again'.

- 高老师已经回家了，你明天再来吧！ Mr Gao has gone home. Why don't you come again tomorrow?

Practice text 16

保护野生动物（一）

两个星期前，我来到印尼的苏门答腊(Sumatra)参加一个环境保护夏令营。

夏令营有一百多个从不同国家来的同学，我们住在一个叫虎村的村子里。因为附近大山里有苏门答腊虎，所以有这个名字。这是一个小村子，从小孩到老人，人口不到八百。我们住在村子旁边的野生动物救护站职员宿舍里。救护站里面的居民都是村民从森林里救来的野生动物，这些动物的妈妈或者已经死了，或者受了严重的伤，不能养他们。

我们每天在救护站试着照顾这些动物，为他们选择早餐和午餐，听老师告诉我们关于野生动物的性格特点。根据他们的介绍，这里的野生动物比以前少了，原因是山里的树木没有以前多，野生植物也不够他们吃，所以生活环境比以前差多了。

1 请阅读课文，然后选择唯一正确的答案。Read the Practice text, and then answer each question by choosing the only correct answer.

i 虎村的人口有
- **A** 八百多
- **B** 七百多
- **C** 九百多

ii 住在救护站的居民是
- **A** 村民
- **B** 野生动物
- **C** 村民的妈妈

iii 我们为动物准备
- **A** 食品
- **B** 家具
- **C** 餐具

iv 野生植物跟以前相比
- **A** 少了
- **B** 多了
- **C** 差不多一样

2 朋友们一起说说应该怎样保护环境。请看图片。Classmates are talking about the best ways to protect the environment. Look at the pictures. 请听录音，选择正确的图片回答问题。Listen, and for each person choose the correct picture.

i 张丽 **ii** 王林 **iii** 李文 **iv** 赵刚 **v** 马云

3 请将下列句子翻译成中文。Translate the following sentences into Chinese using the words provided in the box.

种	选择	破坏	保护	为了	污染
树	花	生活	走路	开车	坐飞机
环境	大自然	动物	海边	山区	市中心

i Pollution is getting more and more serious in many places now.
ii Pollution destroys the environments where many animals live.
iii In order to have a beautiful environment, we must protect nature.
iv We should plant many trees and flowers in city centres and by the sea.
v We should also protect trees in the mountain regions.
vi Everyone should choose not to drive, nor take aeroplanes.
vii My friends and I choose to go to school on foot.

4 扩展练习。Look at the example question and answers below, then write out your own answers to the question given, using the suggestions provided. This exercise can also be used for speaking practice.

	Question	Sample answers
Example:	昨天你是怎么去学校的？ How did you go to school yesterday?	• 昨天我是骑自行车上学的。 • 我也常常走路上学。 • 下雨的时候，妈妈开车送我上学。 • 骑自行车有很多好处，不怕堵车。 • 我也喜欢走路，走路比开车健康。 • 要是天气好，我就走路或者骑自行车上学。 • 走路不但健康，而且有意思， 可以看风景。 • 我常常跟我的同学丽丽一起上学，她是我的邻居。 • 如果街道上没有很多车，空气就很新鲜。 • 我觉得只有大家都努力保护环境，污染才会越来越少。
You do it:	你觉得我们应该多开车还是多走路？ Do you think we should drive more or walk more?	• I feel we should drive less and walk more. • When the weather is nice, we should walk, not drive. • Now there are too many cars on the streets and there are often traffic jams. • If we walk every day, we will be very healthy. • Driving not only pollutes the air, but is also not healthy. • Many people like to drive because it is very comfortable. • When it rains, it is not very comfortable to walk or to ride a bicycle. • Although driving is faster than walking and riding a bicycle, it is expensive. • If there are too many cars in the street, it is not quiet. • If we are in a car, we will not be able to look at the scenery. • I like to walk and look at the scenery at the same time.

5 《学生杂志》想了解同学们对上学方式的意见。请给这家杂志写一篇150个字左右的文章，内容如下：*Student's Magazine* wants to know students' opinions on the ways to get to school. Write about 150 Chinese characters to the magazine. You may include the following:

- 坐车上学有什么好处；
- 走路上学有什么好处；
- 骑自行车上学的好处；
- 你上次骑自行车是在什么时候；
- 你自己最喜欢什么上学方式，为什么。

6 请将下列段落翻译成英文。Translate the following paragraphs into English.

保护野生动物（二）

根据他们的介绍，这里的野生动物比以前少了，原因是山里的树木没有以前多，野生植物也不够他们吃，所以生活环境比以前差多了。保护大自然，保护森林太重要了！那些可爱的动物经过大家的日夜照顾，长得很快！

这里每天都有太阳，很热。我们一有机会就帮助村里的农民种菜。但由于时间的关系，不能天天去帮他们，太可惜了！

三天后就是我们在那里的最后一天，我们都很难过，不想离开那些从早到晚每时每刻为保护野生动物努力工作的职员。我想对他们说："能跟你们一起工作太快乐了！我们一定向你们学习！"

明年我还想再来<u>苏门答腊</u>。

第十七章 旅行

Dialogue A

你在飞机场买票去重庆。You are at an airport buying a ticket to Chongqing. Your teacher acts as the check-in assistant.

shī nǐ yǒu jǐ gè xiāng zi
师：你有几个箱子？
nǐ yí gè hái yǒu yí gè bēi bāo hé yí gè shǒu tí bāo
你：一个。还有一个背包和一个手提包。
shī nǐ yí gè rén lǚ yóu hái shì gēn péng you yì qǐ lǚ yóu
师：你一个人旅游还是跟朋友一起旅游？
nǐ yí gè rén fēi jī jǐ diǎn qǐ fēi
你：一个人。飞机几点起飞？
shī sān diǎn nǐ yǐ qián qù guò chóng qìng ma
师：三点。你以前去过重庆吗？
nǐ qù guò wǒ jīng cháng qù nà lǐ de yí gè qí mǎ jù lè bù
你：去过，我经常去那里的一个骑马俱乐部。
shī nǐ shén me shí hou huí lái
师：你什么时候回来？
nǐ wǔ yuè liù hào
你：五月六号。
shī nǐ jué de zhōng guó de tiān qì zěn me yàng
师：你觉得中国的天气怎么样？
nǐ tài rè le bù guò wú suǒ wèi rú guǒ xí guàn le jiù méi wèn tí
你：太热了，不过无所谓。如果习惯了就没问题。

Dialogue B

你在火车站买票。You are at a railway station buying a ticket to Wuhan. Your teacher is the ticket assistant.

shī nǐ qù nǎr
师：你去哪儿？
nǐ wǒ qù wǔ hàn
你：我去武汉。
shī nǐ yào jǐ zhāng piào
师：你要几张票？
nǐ sān zhāng lái huí piào
你：三张来回票。
shī wǒ men zhǐ mài dān chéng piào nǐ xià wǔ qù hái shì wǎn shàng qù
师：我们只卖单程票。你下午去还是晚上去？
nǐ yào wǎn shàng de piào
你：要晚上的票。
shī nǐ yào ruǎn wò hái shì yìng wò
师：你要软卧还是硬卧？
nǐ yìng wò chē shàng yǒu xǐ liǎn de dì fāng ma
你：硬卧，车上有洗脸的地方吗？
shī yǒu bú guò chē shàng bù néng xǐ zǎo nǐ qù wǔ hàn zuò shén me
师：有，不过车上不能洗澡。你去武汉做什么？
nǐ qù nà lǐ de yí gè jiàn shēn fáng gōng zuò sān gè xīng qī
你：去那里的一个健身房工作三个星期。

Vocabulary

yìng wò	硬卧	hard sleeper
ruǎn wò	软卧	soft sleeper
xiāng zi	箱子	trunk; case
shǒu tí bāo	手提包	handbag
bēi bāo	背包	backpack
xíng li	行李	luggage
lǚ xíng shè	旅行社	travel agent
shì jiè	世界	world
yóu lǎn	游览	to tour
dǎo yóu	导游	tour guide
tiě lù	铁路	railway
dìng piào	订(票)	to book (a ticket)
běn lái	本来	originally; initially
dān chéng piào	单程票	one way ticket
lái huí piào	来回票	return ticket
guó jì	国际	international
guó wài	国外	overseas
qǐ fēi	起飞	to take off
lǚ yóu	旅游	to travel
lù chéng / lǚ chéng	路程/旅程	itinerary

liǎo jiě	了解	to get to know
xué huì	学会	to master
jiě jué	解决	to solve
tí gāo	提高	to improve/ increase
xìng qù	兴趣	interest/hobby
zhèng qián	挣钱	to earn money
shuǐ píng	水平	level; standard
xǐ liǎn	洗(脸)	to wash (face)
xǐ zǎo	洗澡	bath/to bathe
jiàn shēn fáng	健身房	gym
jù lè bù	俱乐部	club
tíng chē chǎng	停车场	car park
wèn hǎo	问好	greetings
fā xiàn	发现	to discover
bú guò	不过	however
qí mǎ	骑马	horse-riding
wú suǒ wèi	无所谓	no matter
zěn me bàn ne	怎么办呢?	What shall we do!
bú jiàn	不见	to disappear

yì jiàn	意见	opinion; complaint
liú lì	流利	fluent
zhī shi	知识	knowledge
děng děng	等等	etc.
dé dào	得到	to obtain; to get
jīng cháng	经常	often
chéng gōng	成功	success(ful)
rú guǒ	如果	if
jí le	……极了	extremely
huí dá	回答	to answer; reply
lǚ kè	旅客	traveller
yóu kè	游客	tourist
pái duì	排队	to queue
shēn qǐng	申请	to apply
lǚ guǎn jiǔ diàn bīn guǎn	旅馆/酒店/宾馆	hotel
yǐn shí	饮食	food and drink
míng shèng gǔ jì	名胜古迹	ancient site and scenic places

chóng qìng	重庆
guǎng zhōu	广州
guì lín	桂林
lā sà	拉萨
nán jīng	南京
tiān jīn	天津
wǔ hàn	武汉
xī ān	西安

Grammar

1 More about using the verb complement

A Here is a summary of the commonly used words.

听见	to hear/heard	看见	to see/saw
做完	to finish doing …	吃饱	to have one's fill
坐下	to sit (seating capacity)	记住	to remember/remembered
买到	to manage to buy/bought	找到	to find/found
考上	to pass/passed the exam for	学会	to master
申请到	to apply for (successfully)	认识到	to realize/realized
走丢	to go missing	学好	to learn well

- 昨天小李的狗走丢了。他们一家人去附近很多地方找了半天，最后在公园旁边的餐馆找到他了。Yesterday, Xiao Li's dog went missing. The whole family went to many places near their home to look for it. In the end they found him in a restaurant next to the park.

B If you want to express the possibility of making progress or completing an action, you can insert 得 between the main verb and the complement.

听得见	can/able to hear	看得见	can/able to see
做得完	can/possible to finish	吃得饱	enough to fill up
坐得下	can sit (enough capacity)	记得住	can remember
买得到	possible to buy	找得到	able to find
考得上	can pass the exam	学得会	able to master

- 这个剧院很大，坐得下五百人。This theatre is huge; it can easily sit five hundred people.
- 虽然日文很难，可是这些学生都很努力，一定学得会。Japanese is very difficult; however, these students are all hardworking, so they will master it.

C If you want to express that it is impossible to make progress or complete an action, you can insert 不 between the main verb and the complement.

听不到	cannot hear	看不到	cannot see
做不完	cannot finish	吃不饱	hunger cannot be satisfied
坐不下	not big enough to sit	记不住	cannot remember
买不到	cannot get hold of/buy	找不到	cannot find
考不上	cannot pass the exam	学不会	unable to master

- 老师，您说太快了，我记不住! Teacher, you said too quickly. I cannot remember it all!
- 在这个商场买不到好手表。This shopping mall don't sell good quality watches.

D If you want to express that progress has not been achieved or an action has failed to be fully completed, you can insert 没 before the main verb.

没听见	failed to hear	没看见	did not see
没做完	did not finish	没记住	did not remember
没买到	failed to buy	没找到	failed to find
没考上	failed the exam	没学会	failed to master

- 哥哥问你问题，为什么不回答？我没听见。Your brother is asking you a question, why don't you answer? I didn't hear him.

2 When you want to name two or more items in a sentence, and neither of them have greater importance than the other, then you can use this structure:

A 除了……以外……还/不但……而且……/也……也……

- Annie speaks both French and German.
  安妮除了法语以外，还会德语。
  安妮不但会说法语，而且会说德语。
  安妮也会说法语，也会说德语。
- I have been to both Guangdong and Hong Kong.
  除了广东以外，我还去过香港。
  我不但去过广东，而且去过香港。
  我也去过广东，也去过香港。

B 一边……一边…… (for doing two things at the same time)

- 很多大学生一边学习一边工作。Many university students take on jobs while studying.
- 每天我一边骑自行车上学一边看风景。 Every day I cycle to school and enjoy the scenery at the same time.
- 我们边走边吃吧！(omitting 一) Let's eat on the road.

C 又……又…… is used for doing many things at the same time or consecutively. It is also used to give a list of similar events.

- 到这里旅游的人又吃，又喝，又唱，又跳，玩儿得开心极了。
  The tourists who came here are having a great time eating, drinking, singing and dancing.

Practice text 17

赵国华是北京一所大学的学生。今年寒假他成功地申请到了导游的工作，这家旅行社在天津。赵国华的普通话很流利，也听得懂上海话和广东话。他最大的兴趣是旅游，不但可以了解世界各地不同的食品，而且还能提高地理知识。除了语言水平高以外，赵国华还有一个健康的身体，另外还学会了做饭。

得到导游的工作，赵国华特别高兴。因为他可以一边挣钱一边游览名胜古迹。他非常喜欢照顾旅客的工作：每天问大家好；回答问题；听他们的意见；发现有订票、酒店房间或者饮食路程方面的难题，就帮助他们解决。这次旅程他们去了西安、桂林和拉萨。

1 请阅读课文，然后回答问题。Read the Practice text and write in Chinese the answers to the questions.

- **i** 这个寒假赵国华为什么不能天天在家？
- **ii** 赵国华为什么喜欢旅游？(给出两个原因。)
- **iii** 导游的工作带来哪些好处？(举出两个例子。)
- **iv** 赵国华在哪些方面要照顾旅客？(举出两个例子。)
- **v** 这次他们去了哪里？(举出一个例子。)

2 请阅读下面的短文。Read the passage.

旅游

现在旅游比以前方便多了，不用出门就可以解决好旅程上的很多问题，比如订火车票、飞机票或者房间等，都可以打电话或者上网，不用去火车站排队了。以前从北京到广州需要坐三天的火车，现在八个多小时就到了。不过风景区的人现在太多了，本来是要看风景的，可是看到的只有人山人海。

请抄写下列句子，选择正确的词语填空。Copy the sentences below and fill in the gap with the correct word from the box.

上网	飞机	风景	三天
火车站	九个	八个	很快

- **i** 从前人们需要去__________排队才能买到火车票。
- **ii** 现在__________就可以订到旅馆的房间。
- **iii** 从北京到广州坐火车最快不到__________小时。
- **iv** 在风景区看到的是很多人，而不是很多__________。

3 李明刚发现他丢了东西，跟导游说话。请看图片。Li Ming has just discovered he has lost something and is talking to the tour guide. Look at the pictures.

请听录音，选择正确的图片回答问题。Listen, and choose the correct picture.

- **i** 李明丢了什么东西？
- **ii** 咖啡馆在哪儿？
- **iii** 李明在厕所的时候，导游去了哪儿？
- **iv** 李明丢东西的时候在做什么？
- **v** 李明从小卖部买了什么？

4 请用表格中给出的短语造句。Write out five sentences or more in your exercise book using the phrases given in the box.

Verb with complement		Suitable objects
认识到	吃得到	一个美丽的公园；很多有用的东西；蓝天和白云；中文学得不太好；美国鸡；法国鸭；当地的马车；会外文的好处；老师说的话；数学作业；飞机票；山下的风景；健康的好处；有名的运动鞋
坐上	买到	
来到	没做完	
看得到	学到	

5 上个暑假你跟一些老师同学一起去了国外旅行。请给笔友写一封150字左右的信。信里说：Last summer holidays, you went abroad to travel with your teacher and classmates. Write your penfriend a letter of about 150 Chinese characters and say:

- 你们去了什么地方，怎么去的；
- 你觉得这个地方的环境怎么样；
- 你对当地人有什么看法；
- 你们都做了些什么；
- 这次旅行最大的收获 (beneficial/benefit) 是什么。

第十八章 节日

Dialogue A

你跟一个中国朋友谈节日。You are chatting to a Chinese friend about festivals.

péng you　nǐ gēn jiā rén dōu qìng zhù nǎ xiē jié rì
朋友：你跟家人都庆祝哪些节日？
nǐ　zhōng qiū jié duān wǔ jié yě yǒu guó wài de
你：中秋节、端午节，也有国外的。
péng you　zhè ge shèng dàn jié nǐ dǎ suàn zài nǎr guò
朋友：这个圣诞节你打算在哪儿过？
nǐ　jīn nián de mù dì dì shì dé guó zài bīng hé shàng diào yú
你：今年的目的地是德国，在冰河上钓鱼！
péng you　qù nián de dà nián chú xī nǐ dōu zuò le xiē shén me
朋友：去年的大年除夕你都做了些什么？
nǐ　zài bìng chuáng shàng kàn bào wǒ de zuǐ zài dǎ qiú de shí hou shòu le shāng yào zhì liáo
你：在病床上看报！我的嘴在打球的时候受了伤，要治疗！
péng you　á bié shāng xīn jīn nián nǐ gēn wǒ qù zhōng guó wán ba
朋友：啊！别伤心！今年你跟我去中国玩吧？
nǐ　tài hǎo le wǒ hěn zǎo jiù xiǎng qù zhōng guó guò nián
你：太好了！我很早就想去中国过年！
péng you　nǐ zuì xiǎng chī de zhōng guó cài shì shén me
朋友：你最想吃的中国菜是什么？
nǐ　bāo zi dòu fu mán tou jiǎo zi chūn juǎn
你：包子、豆腐、馒头、饺子、春卷……

Dialogue B

你跟一位老师谈你在假期做什么。You are chatting to a teacher about what you are going to do on holiday.

lǎo shī　nǐ qù běi jīng zuò shén me
老师：你去北京做什么？
nǐ　wǒ jué dìng qù hú tòng guàng guang nà lǐ de jiàn zhù hěn gǔ lǎo
你：我决定去胡同逛逛，那里的建筑很古老。
lǎo shī　chú le guàng hú tòng hái zuò shén me
老师：除了逛胡同，还做什么？
nǐ　xué běi jīng kǒu yīn wǒ xiǎng yào kǒu yǔ yǒu jìn bù
你：学北京口音，我想要口语有进步。
lǎo shī　nǐ zì jǐ yí gè rén qù hái shì gēn bié rén qù
老师：你自己一个人去还是跟别人去？
nǐ　wǒ zhǎo dào le yí gè lái zì dé guó de xué shēng yì qǐ qù yě ān quán xiē
你：我找到了一个来自德国的学生一起去，也安全些。
lǎo shī　zài běi jīng bù xí guàn chī zhōng guó fàn cài zěn me bàn
老师：在北京不习惯吃中国饭菜，怎么办？
nǐ　běi jīng shāng diàn yě mài wài guó shí pǐn kě kǒu kě lè qì shuǐ suān nǎi děng děng
你：北京商店也卖外国食品，可口可乐、汽水、酸奶等等。
lǎo shī　zhōng guó shāng diàn zài nǎ xiē fāng miàn bǐ yīng guó shāng diàn hǎo
老师：中国商店在哪些方面比英国商店好？
nǐ　zhōng guó shāng diàn hěn wǎn guān mén yīng guó shāng diàn guān mén tài zǎo
你：中国商店很晚关门，英国商店关门太早。

Vocabulary

jié rì 节日	festival	shāng xīn 伤心	sad
chú xī 除夕	New Year Eve	dǎ diàn huà (打)电话	(to call) phone
xīn nián 新年	New Year	míng bai 明白	to understand
lóng 龙	dragon	kě kǒu kě lè 可口可乐	Coca-Cola
guò nián 过年	to celebrate New Year	qì shuǐ 汽水	fizzy drink
guò 过	to spend/to pass (time)	dòu fu 豆腐	tofu
qìng zhù 庆祝	to celebrate	mán tou 馒头	steamed bun
hóng bāo 红包	red packet	suān nǎi 酸奶	yogurt
hú tòng 胡同	alleyway	mǎ shàng 马上	immediately
gǔ lǎo 古老	ancient and old	jiàn jiàn miàn 见/见面	to see/meet up
kāi dǎ kāi 开/打开	to open	cǎi fǎng 采访	interview
guān guān mén 关/关门	to close	hū rán 忽然	suddenly
nián jì nián líng 年纪/年龄	age	jué dìng 决定	to decide/decision
ān quán 安全	safe	fù qián 付钱	to pay
hūn lǐ 婚礼	wedding	kàn bào 看报	to read a newspaper
mù dì dì 目的地	destination	diào yú 钓鱼	line fishing
nuǎn huo 暖和	warm	jìn bù 进步	to improve/progress
qì wēn 气温	temperature	kǒu yǔ 口语	spoken language
liáng kuài 凉快	cool	kū 哭	to cry
bīng 冰	ice	xiào 笑	to laugh
dù 度	degree	kǒu yīn 口音	accent
huá qiáo 华侨	overseas Chinese	zhǎo 找	to look for
zì jǐ 自己	oneself	guà 挂	to hang
lái zì zì cóng 来自/自/从	from	bié 别	don't ...
zhì liáo 治疗	medical treatment	jiā 加	to add
zuǐ kǒu 嘴/口	mouth	yú kuài 愉快	pleasant

Grammar

1 To give sentences a different tone or rhythm, adjectives can be repeated.

高兴 ——	高高兴兴	happy	安静 ——	安安静静	quiet
凉快 ——	凉凉快快	cool	漂亮 ——	漂漂亮亮	beautiful
简单 ——	简简单单	simple	舒服 ——	舒舒服服	comfortable
热闹 ——	热热闹闹	lively	整齐 ——	整整齐齐	tidy
暖和 ——	暖暖和和	warm	干净 ——	干干净净	clean

- 看完电影以后，大家都高高兴兴地回家了。After the film, everyone went home happy.
- 孩子们穿得漂漂亮亮地在公园表演节目。The children dressed up beautifully to perform their programme in the park.
- 我最想舒舒服服地吃一顿中国饭。What I want most is to enjoy a Chinese meal.
- 学生们都在图书馆安安静静地看书。The students are all reading quietly in the library.

2 More about using adverbs

跟/给/用 can be translated as 'to', 'by' and 'in' according to context.

- 下课的时候，老师跟同学们说再见。At the end of the lesson, the teacher said goodbye to the students.
- 昨天妈妈给我寄来一个大邮包。Yesterday my mother sent me a big parcel by post.
- 我们用中文唱歌吧！Let's sing in Chinese!

3 The English words 'if' and 'whether' can be expressed in Chinese by using choice-type questions.

- 他问我**想不想**参加夏令营。He asked me if I wanted to take part in the summer camp.
- 记者问爸爸**可不可以**采访我们一家人。The reporter asked Dad if he/she could interview our family.
- 我们想知道那个外国老师**吃没吃**过饺子。We want to know whether that foreign teacher has eaten dumplings before or not.
- 没有人知道明天**会不会**下雨。No one knows whether it will rain or not tomorrow.

4 带 can team up with 来 and 去 to form 'to bring' and 'to take'.

- 坏了！下雨了！我今天没带伞。Oh no, it's raining. I don't have an umbrella with me today.
- 明天我想带妹妹去看电影。Tomorrow I want to take my sister to see a film.
- 早上老师带来了几本小说给我们看。In the morning, the teacher brought several novels for us to read.

5 More on verb complements that emphasise on movement with 上 (up/on) and 下 (down)

挂：挂上 to hang up　　写：写下 to write down　　关：关上 to close
坐：坐下 to sit down　　穿：穿上 to put on　　吃：吃下 to eat

- 树上边挂上了不同颜色的小灯。There are different coloured lights hanging on the tree.
- 我的电话号码你写下了吗？Did you write down my telephone number?
- 我们都在椅子上坐下吧！Let's all sit on the chairs.
- 天热了！孩子们都穿上了夏天的衣服。It's getting hot now. All the children have put on their summer clothes.

6 Some adjectives can team up with verbs to create new phrases.

好：好看 pretty　　好用 easy to use
好玩儿 funny　　好吃 tasty
难：难看 ugly　　难忘 unforgettable
难走 hard to walk on　　难得 rare
乱：乱丢 to cast off　　乱花 to throw money away
乱说 to talk rubbish　　乱写 to write rubbish
早：早去 to go early　　早回 to come back early
早睡 to sleep early　　早起 to get up early

- 妈妈做的菜都好吃。The dishes that my mother cooks are all tasty.
- 早睡早起是一个非常好的生活习惯。It is a very good life habit to sleep and rise early.

7 To express the degree of emotion or the severity of a situation, use the 得 structure: subject + adjective + 得 + adverb/phrase/sentence.

- 要考试了，学生们忙得很。The exam is coming soon. The students are super busy.

Practice text 18

过年

我叫刘冰，今年春节爸爸决定带我们一家人去新加坡过年。

除夕那天，我们住在市中心的酒店。酒店门口两边挂上了庆祝新春的花灯，漂漂亮亮的。在旁边的教堂里，有一个婚礼刚刚结束。记者在门外采访参加婚礼的客人，相当热闹。

晚上我们去一个华侨开的餐馆吃年夜饭。爸爸很早就打电话订了桌子。我们刚要开始吃饭，厨房马上又为我们上了很多我们没点的特别菜。爷爷看到这些特别菜都是他以前爱吃的，不明白为什么。忽然我们看到餐馆的大厨师对爷爷笑。他就是爷爷四十年没见过面的大学好友。爷爷高兴得哭了。我们大家都高兴得笑了。

吃完了饭，爸爸付了钱，我们一家人高高兴兴地离开了餐馆。晚上我得到了很多红包！那天我们大家都玩得很愉快。

1 请阅读课文，然后选择唯一正确的答案。Read the Practice text, and then answer each question by choosing the only correct answer.

i 记者在哪儿采访？
- **A** 酒店门外
- **B** 教堂门外
- **C** 餐馆外边

ii 什么是特别菜？
- **A** 是我们要的菜
- **B** 是给别人的菜
- **C** 是爷爷做学生时喜欢吃的

iii 爷爷为什么哭了？
- **A** 看到多年以前的老朋友
- **B** 看到我们不高兴
- **C** 没有好吃的菜

iv 谁得到了红包？
- **A** 爷爷
- **B** 爸爸
- **C** 刘冰

2 请阅读下面的短文。Read the passage.

庆祝国庆节

国庆节期间，金星饭店营业时间与以前不同：中午十二点半开门，比以前早半个小时，晚上十一点半关门，比以前晚一个小时。订座十人以上打九折，十五人以上打八折，八岁以下儿童跟两位大人半价用餐，五岁以下儿童跟两位大人用餐不花钱。

请抄写下列句子，选择正确的词语填空。Copy the sentences below and fill in the gap with the correct word from the box.

九个人	十二点	十二点半	十一点半
十点半	十个人	花钱少	给钱

i 金星饭店以前营业时间是从中午__________开始。
ii 金星饭店以前在晚上__________关门。
iii 如果有__________来吃饭价格不比以前便宜。
iv 跟父母来的四岁孩子吃饭不用__________。

3 今天是除夕，你在北京听今后五天的天气预报，请看图片。It is New Year's Eve, and you are in Beijing, listening to the weather forecast for the next five days. Look at the pictures.
请听录音，选择正确的图片回答问题。Listen, and choose the correct picture.

A

B

C

D

E

i 初一　ii 初二　iii 初三　iv 初四　v 初五

4 明明在说他的生日是怎么过的。请看图片。Mingming talks about his birthday activities. Look at the pictures.
请听下面的对话，选择五个正确答案，表明明明做了些什么。Listen, and choose five correct answers to show what Mingming did on his birthday.

A

B

C

D

E

F

G

H

I

5 请用中文写出你在中国城看到了什么。Write five things you see in China town.

6 你刚刚在中国过了一个节日。请给奶奶写一封150字左右的信。信里说：You just celebrated a festival in China. Write a letter of about 150 Chinese characters to your grandma and say:

- 你是跟谁一起过的节；
- 你做了些什么；吃了些什么；
- 你去哪儿玩儿了吗；
- 那个地方怎么样；
- 你喜欢这个节日吗，为什么。

Unit test 3

1 反义词。For each word, find its antonym from the box and write it in your exercise book.

末班车	笑	花钱	死	难过	关	破坏	危险	农村	近
坏处	出	平房	坏	安静	挤	污染	凉快	找到	慢

A 城市 (　　)
B 热闹 (　　)
C 高楼 (　　)
D 好处 (　　)
E 头班车 (　　)
F 空 (　　)
G 干净 (　　)
H 远 (　　)
I 快 (　　)
J 进 (　　)
K 好 (　　)
L 保护 (　　)
M 高兴 (　　)
N 安全 (　　)
O 丢 (　　)
P 生 (　　)
Q 挣钱 (　　)
R 开 (　　)
S 暖和 (　　)
T 哭 (　　)

2 角色扮演。Practise the following role play questions on festivals with your friends.

A 你最喜欢什么节日？
B 上次你跟谁过节？在哪儿？
C 你去过中国的哪个城市？
D 那里的天气怎么样？
E 你明年打算去中国过春节吗？

3 选词填空。Fill in the gap with the correct word given in the box and write the sentences in your exercise book.

别	就	只好	遍	顺着
离	才	不但	次	虽然

A 我一到海边__________想游泳。
B 城里的街道__________常常堵车，而且也不很干净。
C __________小河往南走，不到十分钟就可以看到我以前的小学校。
D 市中心__________你家远吗？
E 吸烟对身体没有好处，只有坏处，__________吸烟了！
F 这本小说你看了几__________了？
G 北京我已经去过三__________了。
H 本来想买海鲜，可是那里的海鲜都卖完了，我们__________买了一条鱼。
I 手机__________贵，可是技术很高，很有用。
J 只有努力学习，考试__________能成功。

4 请阅读下面的短文。Read the passage.

> **年夜饭**
>
> 大年除夕，家家都要吃一顿饺子，欢迎新的一年到来。包饺子是每一个家人都要参加的，大家一边包饺子，一边谈话，快乐极了。除了饺子以外，年夜饭还要有鱼和肉，也有蔬菜，这些都放在饭桌中心，让每个人都吃到。米饭是要每一个人有一碗的。最后喝汤。

抄写下列句子，选择正确的词语填空。Copy the sentences below and fill in the gap with the correct word from the box.

新年	除夕	自己	虽然
大家	人人	一个人	而且

A 年夜饭是在__________的前一天吃的。

B 包饺子是__________都可以参加的活动。

C 年夜饭不但有鱼，__________还有肉和菜。

D 要吃米饭每一个人有__________的碗。

Did you know ...

cháng é bēn yuè
嫦娥奔月

chuán shuō gǔ shí tiān shàng tū rán chū xiàn shí gè tài yáng shài gān le suǒ yǒu
传说古时天上突然出现十个太阳，晒干了所有
de nóng zuò wù bǎi xìng shēng huó tòng kǔ bù kān yí gè míng zì jiào hòu yì de
的农作物，百姓生活痛苦不堪。一个名字叫后羿的
shén jiàn shǒu kàn dào zhè yí qiè yǒng gǎn de shè xià jiǔ gè tài yáng bǎo zhù le
神箭手，看到这一切，勇敢地射下九个太阳，保住了
bǎi xìng de shēng mìng
百姓的生命。

tiān shàng de shén xiān wèi le jiǎng lì tā bǎ liǎng lì cháng shēng bù sǐ de yào
天上的神仙为了奖励他，把两粒长生不死的药
sòng gěi le tā tā bǎ yào jiāo gěi qī zi cháng é bǎo guǎ yǒu yì tiān tā bú zài jiā
送给了他。他把药交给妻子嫦娥保管。有一天，他不在家
de shí hou yí gè huài rén lái tōu cháng shēng bù lǎo yào cháng é wèi le bù ràng tā
的时候，一个坏人来偷长生不老药，嫦娥为了不让他
dé dào yào jiù zì jǐ bǎ yào chī le xià qù méi xiǎng dào tā shēn tǐ biàn de qīng rú
得到药，就自己把药吃了下去。没想到，她身体变得轻如
hóng máo lì kè piāo shàng tiān kōng yì zhí piāo dào le yuè liang shàng
鸿毛，立刻飘上天空，一直飘到了月亮上。

měi nián de bā yuè shí wǔ hào zhōng qiū jié zhè tiān wǎn shàng yuè liàng gé wài
每年的八月十五号中秋节这天晚上，月亮格外
míng liàng rén men yì biān chī zhe yuè bǐng yì biān zhù yuàn měi lì de cháng é kuài kuài
明亮。人们一边吃着月饼，一边祝愿美丽的嫦娥快快
huí dào rén jiān
回到人间。

4 第四单元 高校与工作

Unit 4 Further education and the world of work

中国的名胜古迹 China's historical sites and scenic places

1 Here are some well-known places and landmarks. Can you correctly name each one?

běi jīng	chóng qìng	guì lín	lā sà	shàng hǎi	xī ān
北 京	重 庆	桂 林	拉 萨	上 海	西 安

2 Choose either the Yangtze or Yellow river and do some research about it using the internet or books. Find out some facts such as the length of the river, or the names of any major towns or cities that lie on it.

cháng jiāng 长 江 the Yangtze River	huáng hé 黄 河 the Yellow River

第十九章 高等教育

Dialogue A

你在飞机上，跟一个乘客谈去中国留学。You are on a flight chatting to a passenger about studying in China. Your teacher acts as the passenger.

shī nǐ wèi shén me xiǎng qù zhōng guó liú xué
师：你为什么想去中国留学？
nǐ zhōng guó de gāo děng jiào yù hěn qiáng
你：中国的高等教育很强。
shī nǐ xiǎng qù zhōng guó nǎ ge dì fāng xué hàn yǔ
师：你想去中国哪个地方学汉语？
nǐ shàng hǎi nà shì yí gè yòu nián qīng yòu xiàn dài de chéng shì
你：上海，那是一个又年轻又现代的城市。
shī xué xí hàn yǔ duì nǐ zhǎo gōng zuò yǒu shén me hǎo chù
师：学习汉语对你找工作有什么好处？
nǐ yǒu hěn qiáng de hàn yǔ cái néng zài zhōng guó shùn lì de zhǎo gōng zuò
你：有很强的汉语才能在中国顺利地找工作。
shī nǐ hàn yǔ xué le duō jiǔ le
师：你汉语学了多久了？
nǐ dà gài wǔ nián le xiàn zài hái zài xué
你：大概五年了。现在还在学。
shī zhè shì nǐ dì yī cì qù zhōng guó ma
师：这是你第一次去中国吗？
nǐ dāng rán bú shì wǒ yì bān měi nián dōu qù yí cì zhè shì dì wǔ cì le
你：当然不是，我一般每年都去一次。这是第五次了。

Dialogue B

你在中国的一个书店，跟那里的服务员谈学习汉语。You are in China, in a bookshop, talking to a shop assistant about learning Chinese. Your teacher acts as the assistant.

shī nǐ xiǎng mǎi nǎ zhǒng shū
师：你想买哪种书？
nǐ hàn yǔ pīn yīn bǐ shùn gēn bǐ huà de shū
你：汉语拼音、笔顺跟笔画的书。
shī nǐ de hàn yǔ zhè me liú lì zài nǎr xué de
师：你的汉语这么流利，在哪儿学的？
nǐ xué xiào wèi xué hàn yǔ de xué shēng zhuān mén ān pái le kè
你：学校为学汉语的学生专门安排了课。
shī nǐ jué de wài guó rén xué hàn yǔ zuì dà de kùn nan shì shén me
师：你觉得外国人学汉语最大的困难是什么？
nǐ fā yīn yǔ fǎ shēng diào hé xiě zì gēn yīng yǔ chà hěn duō hěn nán jì
你：发音、语法、声调和写字跟英语差很多，很难记。
shī nǐ dōu yǒu nǎ xiē xué xí fāng fǎ
师：你都有哪些学习方法？
nǐ bāo kuò tīng lì yuè dú xiě zuò kǒu yǔ dōu yào liàn
你：包括听力、阅读、写作、口语，都要练。
shī shàng kè shí lǎo shī zěn me jiāo nǐ men
师：上课时老师怎么教你们？
nǐ tīng xiě shēng cí jù zi hé cí yǔ yě tīng lù yīn zuì hòu gěi dá àn
你：听写生词、句子和词语，也听录音，最后给答案。

Vocabulary

xī wàng	希望	hope; wish
xū yào	需要	to need; to require
yuàn yì	愿意	consent; willing
bú yòng	不用	unnecessary; no need
bù zhǔn	不准	no; not allowed
jiāng yào	将要	to be going to; shall
dà gài	大概	probably
zhuān	专	specialized in; focus
yuè dú	阅读	reading
zhe	着	(grammatical marker)
bì yè	毕业	to graduate; graduation
ān pái	安排	to arrange
bāo kuò	包括	to include
dān xīn	担心	worried
jǐn zhāng	紧张	nervous
mǎn yì	满意	satisfied; satisfying
zháo jí	着急	anxious
xiàn dài	现代	modern
shùn lì	顺利	smooth
yì bān	一般	common; general
dāng rán	当然	certainly; of course
nián qīng rén	年轻(人)	young (people)
bèn	笨	clumsy; stupid
qiáng	强	strong
zhèng què	正确	correct; right
gāo děng	高等	high level; advanced

mù dì	目的	objective; purpose
fā shēng	发生	to happen; to take place
chí chí dào	迟/迟到	to be late
fā yīn	发音	pronunciation
tóng yì	同意	to agree
liú liú zài	留/留在	to remain; to keep; to stay
dá àn	答案	answer
mù qián	目前	at present
jǔ	举	to hold up; to lift
jǔ xíng	举行	to commence; to hold
xiě zuò	写作	(creative) writing
yǔ fǎ	语法	grammar
jù zi	句子	sentence
tīng xiě	听写	dictation
shēng cí	生词	new word
cí yǔ	词语	phrase
pīn yīn	拼音	phonetic writing
bǐ huà	笔画	writing stroke
bǐ shùn	笔顺	stroke order
yǐ wéi	以为	believed (wrongly)
tīng lì	听力	listening
shēng diào	声调	intonation
lù yīn	录音	to record; recording
jì	记	to take notes; to remember

Grammar

1 There are different ways of talking about ongoing actions or situation.

Subject + 正在 / 正 / 在 + verb (phrase) (+ 呢)

- 我们到他家的时候，他妈妈正在做饭。When we arrived at his house, his mother was cooking.
- 学生们正在为考试做准备呢。The students are making preparations for the exam.
- 很晚了，他怎么还在外边坐着？It is very late. How come he is still sitting outside?

Tip

There are four ways to ask 'what are you eating?':

- 你吃什么呢?
- 你正在吃什么?
- 你正吃什么呢?
- 你在吃什么?

2 着 (zhe)

A The word 着 can be used to talk about a situation or state. The word order is:
Location word + verb + 着 + subject/object
Subject/object + verb + 着 + (呢)

- 桌子上放着几本书和一瓶花。There are a few books and a vase of flowers (placed) on the table.
- 看！门外站着一个外国人。Look! There is a foreigner standing outside.
- 这个房子里住着多少人？How many people are living in this house?

B You can add more detail about a main verb in a sentence by using 着 and an additional verb. The word order is: Subject + additional verb + 着… + main verb.

- 邮局不远，我们走着去吧！The post office is not far. Let's walk there.
- 早上他带着狗去公园了。He went to the park with his dog in the morning.

3 从来不/从不 (never) and 从来没……过/从没……过 (have never …)

- 他上学从不迟到。He is never late for school.
- 我上学从来没迟到过。I have never been late for school.
- 我这个朋友从来不吃肉。This friend of mine never eats meat.
- 张先生从来没吃过法国餐。Mr Zhang has never tasted French cuisine before.

4 让 (ràng)

- 请让我来帮助你！Please let me help you!
- 也让他来试试吧！Let him give it a try.

5 用/需要 means 'it needs' or 'there is the need'.

- 从英国坐飞机去美国需要五个小时。It takes five hours to fly from the UK to the USA.
- 我每天走路去学校只用十分钟。It only takes me ten minutes to go to school every day on foot.

不用/不需要 means 'there is no need' or 'does not need to'.

- 在很多国家，去公园不用买票。In many countries, there is no need for anyone to purchase a ticket to visit parks.
- 女儿能自己做饭了，不需要妈妈帮助。The daughter can cook for herself now, so she doesn't need her mother to help.

6 本来 is used mostly as an adverb, meaning 'original/originally'.

- 我们本来以为我们的中文老师是上海人，今天才知道他是日本人。他汉语说得太好了！We had always thought our Chinese teacher was from Shanghai. Not until today did we realize that he is actually from Japan. He speaks Chinese too well!

Practice text 19

王丽丽目前正在努力复习，准备七月的高考。如果考试顺利，她希望去清华大学学习生物。王丽丽从小就不笨，很聪明，三岁就开始上学前班。上课一般从不迟到，每个科目的成绩都让老师们满意。

爸爸本来以为她会愿意去他年轻时读过书的复旦大学，因为那是有名的大学，离他们家又近，所以她妈妈不用太担心。可是女儿不同意，她中学毕业以后不想留在家乡。她要到离家远的地方生活，学会安排自己的生活，不再需要妈妈爸爸的照顾。

星期天学校举行了运动会。王丽丽穿着运动服参加了一百米和八百米赛跑。她妈妈和爸爸来到运动场的时候，她正在准备呢。跑完后，她笑着来到爸爸妈妈身边，一边聊天，一边看比赛，开心极了。

1 请阅读课文，然后选择唯一正确的答案。Read the Practice text, and then answer each question by choosing the only correct answer.

i 王丽丽现在很忙，因为

A 过十八岁的生日。

B 在大学学习生物。

C 马上有很重要的考试。

ii 为什么王丽丽的老师对她很满意？

A 她上学认真努力，学习好。

B 她想去有名的大学。

C 她很聪明。

iii 王丽丽不想去复旦大学，因为

A 爸爸在那个大学学习过。

B 离她的家太近了。

C 妈妈会担心。

iv 王丽丽希望在大学的时候学会做什么？

A 养宠物 **B** 八百米赛跑 **C** 自己照顾自己

2 记者对一名留学生进行采访。请先阅读一下问题。然后根据录音用中文或拼音回答问题。A reporter is interviewing a foreign student studying in China. Listen, and answer the questions. You may write your answers in Chinese characters or Pinyin.

i 记者为什么采访弗兰克？

ii 弗兰克学习什么专业？

[PAUSE]

iii 开始的时候，弗兰克为什么很着急？

iv 老师的安排有什么好处？

3 扩展练习。Look at the example question and answers below, then write out your own answers to the question given, using the suggestions provided. This exercise can also be used for speaking practice.

	Question	Sample answers
Example:	只有学习成绩好才能去大学吗？ Is it true that you can go to a university only if you get good examination results?	• 我觉得要想去好大学，就需要有好成绩。 • 因为有很多学生愿意去好大学，所以他们可以选择要什么样的学生。 • 可是我也觉得我们的学习目的不只是为了上大学。 • 很多大学除了看你的成绩以外，也想知道你是不是有健康的生活方式。 • 当然年轻人应该努力学习，上课不迟到，多读书，包括不同国家的书，知道很多事情。 • 有的学生不想上大学，他们打算很早就工作。 • 虽然有的学生成绩很好，可是没有很多钱，所以也不能上大学。 • 在美国，成绩不好的学生也可以上好大学。
You do it:	你将来希望去中国留学吗？ Do you wish to go and study in China?	• I would love to go to China to study in the future. • I have many Chinese friends and they told me that there are many opportunities in China. • I need to have good examination results in Chinese. • In order to get into a good Chinese university, I need to speak Chinese well, and I also need to read a lot and have good Chinese pronunciation. • I also need to learn Chinese culture and history. • I have already started learning taiji. • I plan to work during the summer holidays, so I can earn money to buy a plane ticket to China. • My friend Mike is in China now. He is studying at Nanjing University. • He also teaches English in a primary school.

4 你的中国笔友想了解一下你的学习计划。请给笔友写一封150字左右的信，信里说：Your penfriend wants to know about your study plans. Write a letter of about 150 Chinese characters and say:

- 今年你学习了哪些科目；
- 明年打算学什么，为什么；
- 你会选择上什么样的大学；
- 为了上你喜欢的大学，你应该做哪些准备。

第二十章 志愿者的工作

Dialogue A

你在地铁站一个很小的日本小吃店，跟中国朋友谈你的周末工作。You are talking about your weekend job with your friend in a Japanese snack bar in an underground station.

péng you　nǐ shì shén me shí hou kāi shǐ zài zhōu mò gōng zuò de
朋友：你是什么时候开始在周末工作的？
nǐ　shàng gè yuè zài yī jiā yǒu míng de rì běn cān guǎn
你：上个月，在一家有名的日本餐馆。
péng you　nǐ dōu zuò xiē shén me
朋友：你都做些什么？
nǐ　xǐ pán zǐ xǐ wǎn ná cài dān bái jiǔ jiàng yóu cù yán píng bēi zǐ
你：洗盘子、洗碗，拿菜单、白酒、酱油、醋、盐瓶、杯子。
péng you　gù kè dōu huì yòng kuài zǐ chī fàn ma
朋友：顾客都会用筷子吃饭吗？
nǐ　yǒu de bú huì yào yòng dāo chā
你：有的不会，要用刀叉。
péng you　zhōu mò yíng yè shí jiān cháng ma
朋友：周末营业时间长吗？
nǐ　hěn cháng dàn shì bú tài tǎo yàn xiǎo fèi huì duō
你：很长，但是不太讨厌，小费会多。
péng you　nà ge rì běn rén gāng gāng jiǎng de huà nǐ tīng de dǒng ma
朋友：那个日本人刚刚讲的话你听得懂吗？
nǐ　dǒng yì diǎnr xiáng xì de yì si jiù bù míng bai le
你：懂一点儿，详细的意思就不明白了。

Dialogue B

你在北京的一家工作介绍所，说你想做的工作。You are in a job agency in Beijing, talking about the kind of work you would like to do. Your teacher acts as your interviewer.

shī　nǐ de gōng zuò dān wèi shì nǎ li
师：你的工作单位是哪里？
nǐ　wǒ xiàn zài bù gōng zuò dàn xī wàng zhǎo yí gè zhì yuàn zhě de gōng zuò
你：我现在不工作，但希望找一个志愿者的工作。
shī　nǐ yǐ qián zuò guò shén me gōng zuò
师：你以前做过什么工作？
nǐ　mì shū hé fú wù yuán yě zuò guò shòu huò yuán hé shòu piào yuán
你：秘书和服务员，也做过售货员和售票员。
shī　nǐ shì nǎ yì suǒ dà xué bì yè de
师：你是哪一所大学毕业的？
nǐ　wǒ gāng cóng běi jīng dà xué bì yè
你：我刚从北京大学毕业。
shī　nǐ dé guò yán zhòng de bìng ma
师：你得过严重的病吗？
nǐ　shí nián qián kāi guò dāo xiàn zài shēn tǐ hěn jiàn kāng
你：十年前开过刀，现在身体很健康。
shī　nǐ wèi shén me xiǎng zuò zhì yuàn zhě
师：你为什么想做志愿者？
nǐ　wǒ xī wàng jiè shǔ jiǎ de jī huì qù lǎo rén yuàn bāng máng
你：我希望借暑假的机会去老人院帮忙。

Vocabulary

qǔ 取	to obtain	jiǎng jiǎng huà 讲 / 讲 话	to speak; speech
qǔ dé 取 得	to achieve	gù shi 故 事	story
qǔ qián 取 钱	to withdraw money	guǎng gào 广 告	advertisement
zhì yuàn zhě 志 愿 者	volunteer	zhuǎn gào 转 告	to pass on
fú wù yuán 服 务 员	service person	guǎng bō 广 播	broadcast
fú wù tái 服 务 台	reception desk	quán 全	entire; whole; all
shòu huò yuán 售 货 员	sales assistant	xiáng xì 详 细	detailed
shòu piào yuán 售 票 员	ticket clerk	kè qi 客 气	polite
mì shū 秘 书	secretary	qí guài 奇 怪	strange; odd; funny
bēi zi 杯 子	cup	shú 熟	familiar with; done
pán 盘	plate	jiè 借	to borrow; to make use of
wǎn 碗	bowl	dāi 呆	to stay
píng 瓶	bottle	tǎo yàn 讨 厌	irksome; annoying
yíng yè shí jiān 营 业 时 间	opening hours	kāi dāo 开 刀	to have surgery
xiǎo fèi 小 费	tip	yì si 意 思	meaning
cài dān 菜 单	menu	xiǎo xīn 小 心	careful
jiàng yóu 酱 油	soya sauce	yàng zi 样 子	appearance; looks
cù 醋	vinegar	gǎn dào 感 到	to feel
dāo chā 刀 叉	knife and fork	dān wèi 单 位	unit (work place)
yán 盐	salt	kě néng 可 能	possibility; possible
kuài zi 筷 子	chopsticks	dǒng 懂	to understand
lǚ xíng 旅 行	to travel	shōu huò 收 获	harvest; gain
ná 拿	to take; to grasp; to hold; to grab	hǎo xiàng 好 像	look like; as if
bāng máng 帮 忙	to help out	yuè lái yuè 越 来 越	more and more
yáo 摇	to shake; to rattle; to rock	yuè yuè 越……越……	the more … the more …

Grammar

1 You have already learnt these compound structures.

挂：挂上　　穿：穿上　　关：关上　　坐：坐下

写：写下　　走：走到　　出：出来　　进：进去

A You can always add 来 or 去 after a verb.

- 上来 to come up　上去 to go up　下来 to come down　下去 to go down
- 进来 to come in　进去 to go in　出来 to come out　出去 to go out
- 过来 to come over　过去 to go over　回来 to come back　回去 to go back

B You can add more verbs such as 跑, 走, 搬, 拿, 写, 放, 取, 看 and 听 and put them before the compound words above.

- 孩子们从外边**跑进来**了。The children ran in from outside.
- 老人从马路对面**走过来**。The elderly person walked across from the other side of the road.
- 我家离学校不远，我可以**走回去**。My home is not far from the school. I can walk back.
- 老师说的话，你都**写下来**没有？Did you write down everything the teacher said?

C The location/destination of the movement can be add after the compound.

- 我们慢慢地走下山去。We slowly walked down the hill.
- 朋友计划五月搬进新家去。My friend planned to move into his new home in May.

2 As mentioned in previous chapters, the Chinese word 是 is mostly used for identification or confirmation, and it is not used in Chinese passive sentences. Below are some sentences that are typically passive in English but not in Chinese.

- 你的历史作业写好了吗？Is your history homework done?
- 不好了！我的钱包丢在上学的路上了。Oh, dear! My purse was lost on the way to school.
- 蛋糕都吃完了吗？Has the cake been eaten?

3 把 structure

A Use the 把 structure to indicate who carried out the action or what result has been achieved. The word order is 'subject + 把 + object + verb + verb complement'.

- 玛丽把晚饭做好了。Mary made the evening meal.
- 你把历史作业写好了吗？Have you done your history homework?
- 不好了！我把钱包丢在上学的路上了。Oh, dear! I lost my purse on the way to school.
- 谁把蛋糕吃了？Who ate the cake?

Tip

Sentences are passive when the most important part is the action, not about the person who carried out that action or when that action took place.

B Verbs such as 放, 挂, 送, 丢, and 留 are often followed by 在 and 给 to talk about what happened or is about to happen.

Sample sentences	✔	✔	✘
I lost the purse on the road.	我把钱包丢在路上了。	钱包丢在路上了。	我丢钱包在路上了。
Please put the book on the desk.	请你把书放在桌子上。	书放在桌子上。	你放书在桌子上。
Hang the map up next to the bed.	把地图挂在床边。	地图挂在床边。	挂地图在床边。
Who do you save the cake for?	你把这块蛋糕留给谁?	这块蛋糕留给谁?	你留这块蛋糕给谁?

C The word order is different in sentences with quantifiers.

Sample sentences	✔	✔	✘
I saw that American film three times.	我把那个美国电影看了三遍。	那个美国电影我看了三遍。	我看了那个美国电影三遍。

D When there is 把 in the sentence, it is referring to something very specific.

Chinese	English
喝茶。	Help yourself to tea!
把茶喝了。	Finish your tea.
在湖边画风景。	Paint scenery by the lakeside.
把湖边的风景画下来。	Paint the lakeside scenery.

Tip

Please wash the clothes clean.

请把这些衣服洗干净。 ✔

请洗这些衣服干净。 ✘

4 The difference between 帮/帮助/帮忙

帮 is a verb and normally needs an object in a sentence.

帮助 is a noun and a verb, and is very flexible in a sentence.

帮忙 is a compound which means 'to help out'. Sometime you can add 个 between these two words.

- 我的中国朋友常常帮我学中文。My Chinese friends often help me with my Chinese.
- 谢谢您的帮助! Thank you for your help!
- 王老师最喜欢帮助他的学生。What Teacher Wang enjoys most is to help his students.
- 姚明今天帮了我们一个大忙。Yao Ming has been a great help today.

Practice text 20

一个志愿者的故事(一)

我叫弗兰克。去年暑假前，我朋友的爸爸在中国工作时看到了一个志愿者活动的广告，他请我朋友转告我，因为他知道我学汉语，一直在找去中国的机会。我把广告里的活动地址写下来，申请写好了以后，就马上寄了过去。又去银行把钱都取了出来。很快，我的申请成功了，机票也买到了。三个星期后，我来到了中国西部的一个小村子。

参加这次活动的志愿者有三十六个中学生，来自不同国家。我们在村子门口下车的时候，看到全村人都走出来欢迎我们，我心里感到特别暖和。

我们在村民的家里住下来，每天跟他们一起吃饭。从早上八点到下午三点我们在一个儿童院帮忙，教村里的孩子们英文，给他们讲故事。

1 请阅读课文，然后回答以下问题。Read the Practice text and answer the questions.

- **i** 弗兰克是怎么知道这个志愿者活动的？
- **ii** 他是怎么去的中国？
- **iii** 这个活动在哪儿？
- **iv** 志愿者都是什么样的人？
- **v** 每天他们在儿童院工作多长时间？
- **vi** 除了讲故事以外，他们还为村里的孩子们做什么？

2 一位记者采访在中国参加夏令营的英国学生安娜。请先阅读一下问题。请听录音，然后用中文或拼音回答问题。A reporter is interviewing Lily, an English student who is at a summer camp in China. Read the questions. Listen, and answer the questions. You may write your answers in Chinese characters or Pinyin.

- **i** 记者为什么采访安娜？
- **ii** 安娜什么时候开始学中文？

[PAUSE]

- **iii** 安娜最喜欢什么活动？
- **iv** 安娜在中国最大的收获是什么？
- **v** 安娜想在哪方面帮助她的老师和同学？

3 讲个故事吧! Story time! Learn the story below and try to tell it to your friends, or alternatively write your own story using the suggestions given in the box.

你的故事 (Your story)	Mike 的故事 (Mike's story)
Last summer holidays, I went to work in a nursery school for three weeks. I taught the children to dance and sing. We also did a lot of activities....	我叫麦克。去年暑假我在一家中国饭馆工作了四个星期，做服务员的工作，洗碗、倒茶。虽然工作很累，可是很有意思。这个工作有很多好处。我每天都会得到小费，也交了很多新朋友。跟我一起工作的人都是年轻人，他们都很友好。要是没有这个工作，我就不能挣钱，不能买很多我喜欢的东西，所以我觉得工作对我的好处很大。我明年打算找一个周末的工作。

4 学生周末应该有工作吗？《中学生网站》要了解一下学生们对周末工作的意见，请给这家网站写一篇150字左右的文章，说说：Should students work at weekends? The Secondary School Students' Website wants to know what students think about working at weekends. Write about 150 Chinese characters and say:

- 你周末工作过吗；
- 中学生周末工作有什么好处，有什么坏处；
- 中学生应该做什么样的周末工作；
- 你在大学周末打不打算工作，为什么。

5 请将下列段落翻译成英文。Translate the following paragraph into English.

一个志愿者的故事(二)

村里的孩子们都很友好，虽然开始的时候他们看上去好像有点儿害怕，都很小心，可能是因为听不懂我的汉语，有时又摇头又摇手，样子很奇怪。时间长了，他们就跟我熟了。我把从英国带来的几包儿童衣服、书和文具送给他们，头上的帽子也给他们了，告诉他们不要客气。他们都高兴得笑了。我们在那里停留了一个星期，我们的汉语也借这个机会越来越好了，还上了当地的新闻广播。我从这次旅行活动中取得的收获真是不小。

第二十一章 娱乐

Dialogue A

你要去中国旅行，给北京一家酒店的经理打电话。You are travelling to China. You are talking on the telephone to the manager of a hotel in Beijing.

jīng lǐ　nín hǎo nín shén me shí hou lái běi jīng
经理：您好！您什么时候来北京？

nǐ　sì yuè jiǔ hào xià wǔ liù diǎn dào
你：四月九号，下午六点到。

jīng lǐ　nín yí gòng yǒu jǐ wèi yào jǐ gè fáng jiān
经理：您一共有几位？要几个房间？

nǐ　wǒ men yí gòng wǔ wèi yào yí gè shuāng rén fáng hé yí gè sān rén fáng
你：我们一共五位，要一个双人房和一个三人房。

jīng lǐ　nín zài běi jīng dāi duō cháng shí jiān
经理：您在北京呆多长时间？

nǐ　sān tiān rán hòu qù xī ān kàn nà li de bīng mǎ yǒng
你：三天。然后去西安看那里的兵马俑。

jīng lǐ　nín jì huà cān guān běi jīng de nǎ xiē míng shèng gǔ jì
经理：您计划参观北京的哪些名胜古迹？

nǐ　yí hé yuán hé gù gōng qù tiān ān mén guǎng chǎng kàn fàng fēng zheng
你：颐和园和故宫，去天安门广场看放风筝。

jīng lǐ　nín xū yào yù dìng qù xī ān de huǒ chē piào ma
经理：您需要预定去西安的火车票吗？

nǐ　bù wǒ huì fā diàn zǐ yóu jiàn zài wǎng zhàn shàng dìng piào
你：不，我会发电子邮件在网站上订票。

Dialogue B

你在北京公共汽车上看中文报，然后碰见一个熟人。You are reading a Chinese newspaper on a bus in Beijing and bump into an acquaintance.

péng you　nǐ xiàn zài qù nǎr
朋友：你现在去哪儿？

nǐ　qù jù chǎng kàn xì rán hòu qù páng biān de jiǔ bā dǎ tái qiú
你：去剧场看戏。然后去旁边的酒吧打台球。

péng you　nǐ zhǔn bèi jǐ diǎn huí lai kàn shí kè biǎo mò bān chē shì shí yī diǎn
朋友：你准备几点回来？看时刻表，末班车是十一点。

nǐ　zhè me zǎo jiù méi chē le bù néng qù le
你：这么早就没车了？不能去了。

péng you　míng tiān gēn wǒ cān jiā jiǔ diàn de pài duì hǎo ma
朋友：明天跟我参加酒店的派对，好吗？

nǐ　wǒ yào qù dǎ bǎo líng qiú ér qiě wǒ méi yǒu wǎn huì lǐng dài
你：我要去打保龄球，而且我没有晚会领带。

péng you　zhōng wén bào zhǐ nǐ kàn de dǒng ma
朋友：中文报纸你看得懂吗？

nǐ　bú tài dǒng dàn shì néng kàn dǒng lián huán huà
你：不太懂，但是能看懂连环画。

péng you　nǐ lái běi jīng duō cháng shí jiān le
朋友：你来北京多长时间了？

nǐ　liǎng nián bàn le wǒ jì huà hòu nián huí guó
你：两年半了，我计划后年回国。

Vocabulary

jiǔ bā	酒吧	bar; pub
tái qiú zhuō qiú	台球/桌球	snooker
bǎo líng qiú	保龄球	bowling
bào zhǐ	报纸	newspaper
huá bīng	滑冰	ice-skating
huá hàn bīng	滑旱冰	skating
huá xuě	滑雪	skiing
huá bǎn	滑板	skateboard
dòng huà piàn	动画片	cartoon
jì lù piān	纪录片	documentary
lián huán huà	连环画	comic
jié mù	节目	programme
kàn xì	(看)戏	(to see) Beijing opera
pái qiú	排球	volleyball
lǐng dài	领带	(neck) tie
yǎn jìng	眼镜	spectacles
wǎn huì	晚会	evening party
pài duì	派对	party
diàn zǐ yóu xì	电子游戏	electronic game
gù shì piàn	故事片	feature film
wǎng zhàn	网站	website
wǎng zhǐ	网址	web address
wǎng mín	网民	web user
wǎng yǒu	网友	web friend
duǎn xìn	短信	text message
liú xíng	流行	trendy/popular
kù	酷	cool
fàng fēng zheng	放风筝	to fly a kite
chū bǎn	出版	to publish
tiào wǔ	跳舞	to dance
dà rén xiǎo hái	大人小孩	old and young
yíng	赢	to win
tōu	偷	to steal
fā	发	to send
pèng jiàn	碰见	to see; to come across
xīn wén	新闻	news
liú yán	留言	message
guǎng chǎng	广场	square
diàn zǐ yóu jiàn	电子邮件	e-mail
bié rén	别人	other people
bèi	被	(passive voice)
shǒu tí diàn nǎo	手提电脑	laptop
jì huà	计划	to plan/plan
xià jiàng	下降	to decrease/fall
gāng cái	刚才	just now
tǐ cāo	体操	gymnastics
shí kè biǎo	时刻表	timetable
cān guān	参观	to visit; to tour; to look at
tiào	跳	to jump
huán shū qián	还(书/钱)	to return (books/money)
běi hǎi gōng yuán	北海公园	Beihai Park
bīng mǎ yǒng	兵马俑	Terracotta Army
cháng chéng	长城	the Great Wall
gù gōng	故宫	the Palace Museum
tiān ān mén	天安门	Tian'anmen square
tiān tán	天坛	the Temple of Heaven
xī hú	西湖	the West Lake
yí hé yuán	颐和园	the Summer Palace

Grammar

1 被, 让 and 叫 structure

A The 被 structure is probably closest to the English passive sentence. If we call the subject 'receiver' for being on the receiving end of the action, and someone/something that issues the action 'doer', the word order will look like:

The receiver + 被 + doer + completed action (verb with complement)

'被 + doer' is the equivalent of 'by + someone/something' in English and always goes before the action, not at the end of the sentence as in English.

Please note that other words such as time reference may be put before 被 and the subject (receiver) may be omitted.

- 小王呢？他刚才被地理老师叫到办公室去了。Where is Xiao Wang? He was called into the office by the Geography teacher just now.
- 你买的新小说可以借给我看看吗？对不起，已经被别的朋友借走了。Could you lend me the new novel you bought? Sorry, it has already been lent to other friends.

The receiver + 被 + completed action (verb with complement)

被 is the equivalent of 'to be' in English if the 'doer' is not mentioned.

- 花瓶被打坏了！The vase was broken!

While 被 is for both written (formal) and colloquial (informal) usage, 让 and 叫 are mostly used for everyday situations only and they must be followed by a 'doer'. They cannot be put directly before verbs, and 给 sometimes follows the 'doer'.

- 你又让老师说了吧？You were told off by your teacher again, weren't you?
- 我那杯茶叫谁给喝了？Who drank my tea?

B When the 把 and 被 structures or the passive voice are used in Chinese, they all have the same effect on word order; in each case the object moves and is placed before the verb. This is done to allow the verb to be adapted or added to in many ways according to how much information is to be given, for example to give directions, to explain results, or to express the extent of an action. Colloquial Chinese can go even further by putting the object/topic of discussion at the very beginning for almost all types of sentences, which is referred to as the topic-comment structure.

- 今天的作业你做完了吗？Have you finished today's homework?
- 那辆自行车他已经卖了。He has already sold that bicycle.
- 这本书我看了五遍了，可是还想再看。I have read this book five times and want to read it again.

2 For question words such as 什么时候, 什么, 哪儿, 谁, 怎么, 多少/几, we can add 都 after them for inclusion, 都不 or 也不 for exclusion and 过 or 没 for what has or has not completed. They can be translated into 'everything, everywhere, everyone, any time, nobody, whichever way, no time, nothing, anything, anywhere ...'.

- 现在在网上什么都能买到。One can buy everything online nowadays.
- 他肚子不舒服，什么都不想吃。He has a pain in his stomach; he does not want to eat anything.
- 她不喜欢旅行，除了家乡，几乎哪儿也没去过。She does not like travelling. She has been to nowhere apart from her home town.

When question words follow the verbs in a negative sentence, the meanings are mostly 'anything', 'anywhere', 'anyone'.

- 很多人不买什么，只是看看。Many people are not buying anything but only looking.
- 你去哪儿？我不去哪儿。到外边走走。Where are you going? I am not going anywhere. I'm just having a walk outside.

3 这么 (as ... as this) and 那么 (as ... as that) can both be simply translated as 'so', and 怎么 means how/how come/how on earth.

- 怎么这么热？现在才是三月。How come it is so hot? It is only March!
- 丢了这么多钱，怎么办？What are we going to do losing so much money?

4 刚 (just) and 刚才 (just now/short while ago)

- 他刚回家就又出去了。He went out again no sooner than he came home.
- 刚才谁给我们打电话了？Who called us just now?

5 The very useful word 开 has many meanings as a verb: to open, to turn on, to drive (a car), to commence (a meeting), to operate (in surgery) and so on. Its opposite is 关: to close, to shut, to turn off and so on. These two words are frequently used with a main verb or following 去 or 来.

- 我不喜欢关着窗户睡觉。I do not like sleeping with the windows closed.
- 他每天开车上班。He drives to work every day.
- 弟弟要开灯看书。My brother wants to turn on the light to read.

When they are the main verbs of a sentence, however, they need verb complements to complete the action.

打开　开开　开着　开了　关上　关掉　关了

- 快！打开门。Quickly, open the door!
- 请把门关上。Please close the door.
- 电视关掉了吗？Has the TV been turned off?

Practice text 21

手机的好与坏

现在手机越来越流行，大人小孩差不多都有。有人每年都换新式手机，觉得很酷。手机的好处跟坏处，网民们有不同的意见。

林海说："去不熟的地方，打开手机看上面的地图就不会迷路了。借的书要还了，手机也能告诉我们，什么都能做。"

小美说："手机上有动画片、故事片等娱乐节目，还可以看到新闻和纪录片等教育节目。"

小明说："碰见了坏人，手机就很容易被他们偷去。"

赵方说："太多学生把时间发短信和电子游戏上。成绩下降了，眼睛也不好了，要戴眼镜。我们应该多去外面做活动，夏天去跳跳舞，去公园滑滑板，冬天去滑滑雪、滑滑冰。"

我觉得这些活动都太危险，更喜欢呆在房间里用电脑滑电子旱冰。

1 请阅读课文，然后回答以下问题。Read the Practice text and answer the questions.

- **i** 手机在哪两个方面帮助了林海？
- **ii** 小美说手机上可以看什么节目？(举出两个例子。)
- **iii** 小明担心坏人会做什么？
- **iv** 赵方说手机对学生的健康有什么坏处？
- **v** 赵方说冬夏两季有哪两种不同的活动？

2 朋友们一起谈他们在手提电脑上做什么。请看图片。Friends are talking about what they use their laptops for. Look at the pictures.
请听录音，选择正确的图片回答问题。Listen, and choose the correct picture.

A

B

C

D

E

F

G

i 兰花 **ii** 东东 **iii** 小京 **iv** 小红 **v** 小海

3 讲个故事吧！Story time! Read the story below and try to tell it to your friends, or alternatively write your own story using the vocabulary provided in the box.

你的故事 (Your story)		王明的故事
pà 怕	to fear/be afraid	昨天早上，在去学校的路上，我跟朋友李丽看到一个五六岁的小女孩儿在马路旁边哭。因为她前后左右都没有大人，所以我们觉得很奇怪。 李丽问我："我们应不应该帮她呢？" 我觉得应该帮她，因为她在路边会有危险。所以我们就给999打了电话。对小女孩儿说不要怕。 很快，警车来了。警察走过来，他们后边跟着一位年轻的太太。 小女孩儿看到那个太太，高兴地跑过去，那个太太抱着小女孩儿开心地哭起来。她走过来对我们说："谢谢你们！" 警察也对我们说谢谢。 那天我们虽然上课迟到了，可是老师没有说我们，因为我们做了一件好事。
wēi xiǎn 危险	danger	
jiù hù chē 救护车	ambulance	
xīn zàng 心脏	heart	
wèn tí 问题	problem	
yán zhòng 严重	serious	
zuò zài dì shàng 坐在地上	to sit on the ground/floor	
wèn tā 问他	asked him	

4 你们学校新来了一个外国留学生，上个周末你跟他/她在公园散步，看到一个老人忽然病了。请用中文写150字左右，说说：A foreign student comes to your school. Last weekend, you went for a walk in the park with him/her and saw an old man fall sick suddenly. Write about 150 Chinese characters and say:

- 你觉得应该怎么做；
- 留学生跟你说了什么；
- 后来发生了什么事。

第二十二章 计划将来

Dialogue A

你跟中国朋友谈中学毕业以后的计划。You are discussing your plans after high school graduation with a Chinese friend.

péng you 朋友：nǐ jì huà qù dà xué jì xù xué xí ma 你计划去大学继续学习吗？

nǐ 你：wǒ fù mǔ ràng wǒ dú kuài jì shī zhuān yè dàn wǒ xiǎng xiū xué yì nián 我父母让我读会计师专业。但我想休学一年。

péng you 朋友：nǐ yǒu chū guó de dǎ suàn ma 你有出国的打算吗？

nǐ 你：méi yǒu wǒ xiǎng gǎn zhe zhèng qián xiān zhèng xiē xué fèi 没有，我想赶着挣钱，先挣些学费。

péng you 朋友：nǐ zuì xiǎng zuò de gōng zuò shì shén me 你最想做的工作是什么？

nǐ 你：sī jī kāi jiù hù chē 司机，开救护车。

péng you 朋友：wèi shén me xiǎng zuò zhè ge gōng zuò 为什么想做这个工作？

nǐ 你：wǒ xǐ huan bāng zhù bié rén tè bié shì zài kùn nan zhōng de rén 我喜欢帮助别人，特别是在困难中的人。

péng you 朋友：nǐ xià tiān chú le zhèng qián yǐ wài xiǎng qù nǎr wánr ma 你夏天除了挣钱以外，想去哪儿玩儿吗？

nǐ 你：měi guó kàn kan lǎo ye tā zài nàr zuò lǜ shī 美国看看姥爷，他在那儿做律师。

Dialogue B

你准备出国找工作，在跟中文老师谈话。You intend to find work abroad. You are talking to your Chinese teacher.

lǎo shī 老师：nǐ xiàn zài zài zhǎo shén me yàng de gōng zuò 你现在在找什么样的工作？

nǐ 你：gōng chéng shī kě shì zhè lǐ zhǐ yǒu shí pǐn chǎng xū yào gōng rén wǒ xiǎng chū guó shì shi 工程师，可是这里只有食品厂需要工人。我想出国试试。

lǎo shī 老师：nǐ yào qù nǎ lǐ 你要去哪里？

nǐ 你：dà gài xiāng gǎng huò zhě xīn jiā pō 大概香港或者新加坡。

lǎo shī 老师：nǐ wèi shén me yào xuǎn zé qù nà liǎng gè dì fang 你为什么要选择去那两个地方？

nǐ 你：wǒ bà ba zài xiāng gǎng dà xué zuò guò jiào shòu yě qù guò xīn jiā pō 我爸爸在香港大学做过教授，也去过新加坡。

lǎo shī 老师：nà lǐ de qì hou nǐ néng xí guàn ma 那里的气候你能习惯吗？

nǐ 你：tīng shuō hěn rè bú guò zhù jiǔ le jiù néng xí guàn le 听说很热，不过住久了就能习惯了。

lǎo shī 老师：nǐ xǐ huan chī dōng nán yà de cài ma 你喜欢吃东南亚的菜吗？

nǐ 你：wǒ lǎo lao huì zuò yà zhōu cài suǒ yǐ wǒ duì yà zhōu cài hěn shú 我姥姥会做亚洲菜，所以我对亚洲菜很熟。

Vocabulary

dài fu	大夫	doctor
gōng chéng shī	工程师	engineer
gōng rén	工人	labourer; worker
jiào shòu	教授	professor
lǜ shī	律师	lawyer
kuài jì shī	会计师	accountant
sī jī	司机	driver; chauffeur
dāng	当	to work as (profession)
gǔ diǎn yīn yuè	古典音乐	classical music
yīn yuè huì	音乐会	concert
fù qīn	父亲	father
mǔ qīn	母亲	mother
lǎo ye	姥爷	maternal grandpa
lǎo lao	姥姥	maternal grandma
qīn ài de	亲爱的	dear
ràng	让	to allow; to let; to make
chū shì gù	(出)事故	(to have an) accident
chē huò	车祸	car accident
jiǎo	脚	foot
jiù hù chē	救护车	ambulance
yǎn chū	演出	performance
biǎo yǎn	表演	to perform
yǎn yuán	演员	actor; actress
chū shēng	出生	to be born
tǐ zhòng	体重	body weight
tuǐ	腿	leg
dòng zuò	动作	motion; movement
kōng tiáo	空调	air-conditioning
mó tuō chē	摩托车	motorbike
dà shī	大师	master
nuǎn qì	暖气	heating
bīng xiāng	冰箱	refrigerator
gǎn	赶	to hurry; to catch up; to drive
xué fèi	学费	school fee
hé zi	盒子	box
ǎi	矮	short (height)
dī	低	low
hòu	厚	thick
píng	平	even; level; flat
xíng	行	fine; OK
yuán	圆	round; circle
zhí	直	straight
jiē	接	to receive; to meet
lái xìn	来信	to write; to send a letter
wǔ shù	武术	martial art
tǎng	躺	to lie down
liú xià	留下	to leave … with; to give
shēn kè	深刻	deep; to profound
yìn xiàng	印象	impression
bú guò	不过	but; however
zhǐ yào … jiù	只要……就	as long as
bìng qiě	并且	also; as well
jié hūn	结婚	to get married

Grammar

1 Describing someone's appearance in Chinese is mostly done with adjectives. Duplication of characters is also common, along with the verbs 有 (to have) and 长得 (to grow into/look) or 看上去 (to look/seem).

- 明丽有黑黑的眼睛，长长的头发，白白的皮肤。Mingli has dark eyes, long hair, and fair skin.
- 她看上去不算老，大概在五十岁上下。She does not look very old, about in her fifties.

2 The expression '不到 + time reference + 就……' / 'time reference +不到 + 就……' can be translated as 'within … already …' or 'before'.

- 她不到十岁就开始在剧院表演武术了。Before reaching the age of ten, she had already started to perform martial arts in the theatre.
- 他常常九点不到就想上床睡觉。He often wants to go to bed before nine o'clock.

3 The expression '一点儿也不(没)/一点儿都不(没)' can be translated as '... not … at all'.

- 我的汉语一点儿也不好！My Chinese is not good at all.
- 中午饭他一点儿都没吃。He did not eat any lunch at all.
- 我一点儿也不怕他。I am not in the least bit afraid of him.

4 印象 (impression) is a noun, and is often teamed up with the verbs 留下, 有 or 给.

- 那些可爱的孩子们给我留下了很深的印象。Those lovely children left a deep impression on me.
- 那个城市给你的印象怎么样？What is your impression of that city?
- 你对这次旅行有什么印象？What is your impression of this trip?

5 When 当 is combined with place or time words, it means 'that'.

当地 – local

当时 – at the time (when event takes place)

当天 – on the day of the event.

我是去年九月一号第一次见到他的。他当天就对我说，我们结婚吧！当时我不知道怎么回答他才好，就什么也没说。后来他带我去当地的一家电影院看了一场电影。看完电影以后就都回自己的家了。他忘了问我的电话号码，我也忘了问他的电话号码。It was on the 1st of September last year that I met him for the first time. He asked me on that very day if we could get married. At the time, I did not know how to answer him, so said nothing. Later on, he took me to a local cinema and we watched a film there. After the film, we each went home separately. He forgot to ask for my phone number, and I forgot to ask for his.

当 can also team up with ……的时候 to emphasise a particular moment in the past.

当他们结婚的时候，两个人都没有房子。(emphasizing the time when they were married)

6 The difference between 只要……就 and 只有……才 depends on the meanings of 就 and 才.

- 只要能吃得到饺子，我这个春节就过得满意了。As long as I can have dumplings, I will be satisfied with the Spring Festival.
- 只有到了少林寺，才能见到真正的武术。Until you have arrived at Shaolin Temple, you will not understand real martial arts.

Practice text 22

张小强生活在广州郊区。他长得不矮，厚厚的头发，圆圆的眼睛，腿直直的。他十五岁就离开了家，去香港学武术。三年后，他回广州，在一座庙里开了一个武术班。不久剧院的经理开始请他去表演。他的演出总是大受欢迎，因为张小强的武术水平真是一点儿也不低，并且手脚快得像电影里的一样，常常给大家留下了深刻的印象。

有一天，他接到北京电影厂的来信，说他们正在找一个武术演员。请他去电影厂试试，看看他身高、体重、样子都行不行。很快张小强当上了演员，演一个会骑摩托车的武术大师。他姥姥害怕他会出事故和车祸，常常担心，以后就不看他的电影了。

刚刚二十岁的他就给亲爱的家人买了大房子，里面空调、暖气、冰箱和家具都全。邻居都说，"只有住上了外孙子买的楼，才知道外孙子的好处。"

1 请阅读课文，然后选择唯一正确的答案。Read the Practice text, and choose the only correct answer.

i 张小强从香港回来的时候有多大？

A 十五岁

B 十六岁

C 十八岁

ii 他回到家乡后，开始做什么工作？

A 电影演员

B 武术教师

C 剧院经理

iii 姥姥为什么为张小强担心？

A 武术动作太难

B 摩托车太快

C 怕有危险

iv 张小强为家人买的房子怎么样？

A 设施很全

B 没有衣柜

C 邻居可以住

2 记者对武汉中学生古典音乐比赛第一名的马英进行采访。先阅读一下问题。请听下面的采访，用中文或拼音回答问题。A reporter is interviewing the winner of the Wuhan Secondary School Classical Music Competition, Ma Ying. Listen, and answer the questions. You may write your answers in Chinese characters or Pinyin.

i 记者为什么采访马英？

ii 马英是怎么喜欢上古典音乐的？

iii 花是谁送的？

[PAUSE]

iv 马英有什么学习方法？

v 为了考大学，除了音乐好以外，什么也很重要？

3 扩展练习。Look at the example question and answers below, then write out your own answers to the question given, using the suggestions provided. This exercise can also be used for speaking practice.

	Question	**Sample answers**
Example:	你觉得年轻人为什么要学习？	• 我们每个人都应该学习。 • 要是我学习学得好，我就会有好成绩。 • 要是我有好成绩，就可以上好大学。 • 要是我是大学生，就能找到一个好工作。 • 要是我有一个好工作，我就能挣很多钱。 • 要是我挣很多钱，我就能买到很多好东西。 • 要是我有很多好东西，我就把它们送给我的家人和朋友。 • 我的家人和朋友看到这些好东西，他们就会很开心。 • 看到家人和朋友很开心，我就会高兴得不得了。
You do it:	你为什么想去中国？	• I have always liked Chinese culture since I was little. • If I learn Chinese well, I can go to a Chinese university. • If I can go to China, I will be able to talk to Chinese people in Chinese, read Chinese books and watch Chinese films. • If I can find a job in China, I can invite my family and friends over. • If my friends come to China to see me, I can take them to see the Great Wall of China and cook Chinese food for them.

4 你的小学老师想知道你对将来有什么打算。请写一封150字左右的信给

他/她，信里说：Your primary school teacher wants to know your future plans. Write a letter of about 150 Chinese characters and say:

- 你觉得你应该上大学吗，为什么；
- 你父母对你的计划有什么意见；
- 你对什么工作最感兴趣，为什么；
- 朋友对你喜欢的工作有什么看法。

第二十三章 理想的工作

Dialogue A

你跟一个中国老师谈什么工作最理想。You are chatting about ideal jobs with your Chinese teacher.

lǎo shī　　nǐ jué de shén me shì zuì lǐ xiǎng de gōng zuò
老师：　你觉得什么是最理想的工作？

nǐ　　yí gè rén de zhí yè shì tā de yè yú ài hào　jiù zuì lǐ xiǎng
你：　一个人的职业是他的业余爱好，就最理想。

lǎo shī　　nǐ zuì xiǎng zuò de gōng zuò shì shén me
老师：　你最想做的工作是什么？

nǐ　　wǒ de xìng gé bǐ jiào ān jìng　xiǎng zài rén shǎo de dì fāng gōng zuò
你：　我的性格比较安静，想在人少的地方工作。

lǎo shī　　nǐ jì huà jiāng lái shēn qǐng shén me gōng zuò
老师：　你计划将来申请什么工作？

nǐ　　zài měi shù guǎn　fù zé zhǎn lǎn pǐn de ān pái
你：　在美术馆，负责展览品的安排。

lǎo shī　　wèi shén me xuǎn zé měi shù guǎn
老师：　为什么选择美术馆？

nǐ　　wǒ xǐ huan huà huà　gèng xǐ huan kàn huà
你：　我喜欢画画，更喜欢看画。

lǎo shī　　nǐ xiǎng qù nǎ gè dà xué
老师：　你想去哪个大学？

nǐ　　lún dūn dà xué měi shù xì
你：　伦敦大学美术系。

Dialogue B

你跟一个中国朋友谈你将来的理想。You are discussing your future aspirations with a Chinese friend.

péng you　　nǐ duì jiāng lái dōu yǒu nǎ xiē jì huà
朋友：　你对将来都有哪些计划？

nǐ　　wǒ xī wàng néng yǒu gè hǎo gōng zuò　bù xiǎng zǎo jié hūn
你：　我希望能有个好工作，不想早结婚。

péng you　　hǎo gōng zuò róng yì zhǎo ma
朋友：　好工作容易找吗？

nǐ　　yào zì jǐ nǔ lì　yě yào yùn qì hǎo
你：　要自己努力，也要运气好。

péng you　　nǐ duì jiāng lái de zhàng fū yǒu shén me yāo qiú
朋友：　你对将来的丈夫有什么要求？

nǐ　　shēn tǐ hǎo　xìng qíng hǎo　xǐ huān xiǎo hái zi
你：　身体好，性情好，喜欢小孩子。

péng you　　yǒu le hái zi yǐ hòu hái xiǎng gōng zuò ma
朋友：　有了孩子以后还想工作吗？

nǐ　　wǒ huì jì xù gōng zuò
你：　我会继续工作。

péng you　　nǐ de péng you men yǒu zhè yàng xiǎng ma
朋友：　你的朋友们有这样想吗？

nǐ　　shì de　hěn duō rén rèn wéi gōng zuò hé jiā tíng tóng yàng zhòng yào
你：　是的，很多人认为工作和家庭同样重要。

Vocabulary

zhǎn lǎn 展览	exhibition
gōng sī 公司	company
yàn huì 宴会	banquet
zhí yè 职业	career
yóu dì yuán 邮递员	postman
shòu yī 兽医	vet
lǎo bǎn 老板	boss
yá yī 牙医	dentist
yùn qì 运气	luck; fortune
méi xiǎng dào 没想到	unexpectedly
xì 系	faculty
xìng qíng 性情	nature; disposition
shàng bān 上班	to go to work
xià bān 下班	to finish work
zhǔn shí 准时	on time
jì shù 技术	skill; technology
kè wài huó dòng 课外活动	extra-curricular
yāo qiú 要求	request
bàn lǐ 办理	to deal; to handle
cún qián 存钱	to save money
yǐ wài 以外	besides
zì tiáo 字条	written note
dì xià shì 地下室	basement
dān zi 单子	list
máo dùn 矛盾	conflict; contradiction
rén wù 人物	character; figure
shì qing 事情	matter
guāng pán 光盘	disc; CD
xià zǎi 下载	to download
háng kōng fú wù yuán 航空服务员	flight attendant
qīng nián 青年	youth
jiā tíng 家庭	family
yè yú 业余	amateur; spare time
yāo qǐng 邀请	to invite
lǐ fà 理发	haircut
shēng qì 生气	angry
fù zé 负责	responsible; in charge
zhuān yè 专业	profession; speciality
yě xǔ 也许	perhaps; maybe
jiāo péng you 交朋友	to make friends
chuāng hu 窗户	window
shū zi 梳子	comb
máo jīn 毛巾	towel
jìng zi 镜子	mirror
pāi zhào zhào xiāng 拍照/照相	to take a photo/picture
lǐ xiǎng 理想	ideal; aspiration
àn zhào 按照	according to; following

Grammar

1 Although the word 受 actually means 'receive', it is translated differently depending on the situation.

- 他们全家人从老到小都受过大学教育，这在我们村里是很难得的。Everyone from old to young in their family went to university. This is rare in our village.
- 我受的伤不严重，明天就可以上班了。The injury I had is not serious and I am able to go to work tomorrow.
- 成龙的电影在美国特别受欢迎。Films by Jackie Chan are popular in America.

2 The difference between 越来越…… and 越……越……

A word order: 越来越 + verbs of emotions such as 喜欢/爱/想

- 我越来越喜欢学汉语了。I like to learn Chinese more and more.

B word order: 越来越 + adjective

- 李明天天运动，身体越来越健康。Li Ming exercises every day and his body is getting healthier and healthier.
- 经过努力，哥哥的学习成绩越来越好了。With hard work, my brother's examination results are getting better and better.

C word order: 越 + part A + 越 + part B, and part B is the result of part A.

- 天气越热我越舒服。The hotter the weather gets, the more comfortable I feel.

3 The difference between 先……(然)后…… (first ..., then ...) and 先……后来…… (first ..., then/later/later on ...)

A 先……(然)后 (first ..., then ...) emphasizes that there is a conditional relationship between two events, and can be accompanied by 才 or 再.

- 你要先吃饭，后看电视，不可以先看电视，后吃饭。You need to eat first and then watch TV. You cannot watch TV before you eat.
- 他们先在公园玩了一会儿篮球，然后才回家。They played basketball for a little while before they went home.

B 先……后来 (first ..., later on ...) explains a sequence of events in the past.

- 王小姐先在一个大公司工作了两年，后来决定去学校工作。Miss Wang worked in a big company for two years. Then she decided to work in a school.
- 他先去了美国一个大学读化学专业，后来就回国了。He first went to study chemistry in an American university. Later he came back home.

C The difference between 后来 (later) and 以后 (from now on/after)

- 他后来去了一个大城市工作。Later, he went to work in a big city.
- 我们以后别去饭馆吃饭了，把钱花在旅游上吧。Let's not eat out in restaurants from now on and spend the money on travelling.
- 中学毕业以后，他跟朋友去农村参加了一个夏令营。After graduating from high school, he went to take part in a summer camp in the countryside with his friends.

4 没想到 indicates something that has not been thought of previously, which is unexpected or out of the blue.

- 我们本来决定星期天去公园吃野餐，没想到那天下雨了。We originally decided to have a picnic in the park on Sunday; lo and behold it rained that very day!
- 老张的手表已经丢了两个星期了。没想到今天警察把表送上门来。Lao Zhang has lost his watch for two weeks now. Out of the blue, the police delivered the watch to his door today.
- 我真没想到物理考试会考得这么差！I really did not expect to do so badly in my Physics exam!

Practice text 23

做自己的老板（一）

2000年，不到十七岁的马世明考上了牙科大学，这在他家是历史上第一次。他的爷爷奶奶不认字，父亲母亲也只受过中小学教育。四年后，小马在城里当上了挣钱不少的牙医。全家人都为他感到特别高兴。

可是没想到，刚工作不到两个月，小马忽然对他的父母说，他心里已经矛盾了很久了，因为他发现每天早九晚五的生活不是他想要的。他想把时间花在自己喜欢做的事情上，做自己的老板。

离开了牙医工作以后，小马在家里的地下室学起理发技术来。母亲开始的时候对他有一点儿生气，觉得丢掉牙医那么好的工作太可惜了。可是他父亲越想越觉得儿子做得对。

1 请阅读课文，然后回答以下几个问题。Read the Practice text and answer the questions.

- **i** 马世明家人的教育情况怎么样？（举出两个例子。）
- **ii** 小马当上牙医的时候有多大？
- **iii** 小马做了多长时间的牙医？
- **iv** 他不想继续当牙医的原因有哪两个？
- **v** 马世明在什么地方开始了他的新工作？
- **vi** 他妈妈为什么对他生气？

2 朋友们在一起谈他们理想的工作。Friends are talking about their ideal jobs. Look at the pictures.

请听录音，选择正确的图片回答问题。Listen, and choose the correct picture.

i 兰兰　**ii** 小东　**iii** 京京　**iv** 小黄　**v** 小李

3 请用中文写出你在一家旅馆看到什么。Write five things you see in a hotel.

4 一位名人到你的学校给你们上了一节课，请写一篇150字左右的文章，内容包括：A famous person gave a speech in your school. Write about 150 Chinese characters. You may include the following points:

- 他/她是谁，为什么有名；
- 在课上他/她跟你们说了什么；
- 下课以后他/她跟你们做了什么；
- 你喜欢他/她吗，为什么。

5 请将下列段落翻译成英文。Translate the following paragraph into English.

做自己的老板（二）

父亲把存在银行里的五万块钱取出来，给儿子拿去买理发用具：梳子、毛巾、镜子等等。小马从网上下载了一些理发技术的课程，又买了理发教学光盘，白天黑夜地学习当时最流行的发式做法。小马在学校的时候，就喜欢参加各种课外活动，技术上的东西一学就会。

妈妈后来也明白了儿子的想法，天天来帮忙。小马先把需要的东西写在字条上，然后请母亲按照单子去商店买。不到一年，马世明的理发店就出名了，顾客越来越多，包括一些当地的名人。这件事让他变成了当地的新闻人物。新闻记者多次来采访了他，邀请他们全家拍照，上了报纸和电视。

第二十四章 外面真美丽

Dialogue A

你跟签证办理处用电话进行对话。You are talking to a visa application agent on the phone. Your teacher acts as the agent.

shī wèi nǐ hǎo shēn qǐng qiān zhèng de wén jiàn zhǔn bèi hǎo le ma
师：喂，你好！申请签证的文件准备好了吗？
nǐ zhǔn bèi hǎo le bāo kuò wǒ de hù zhào
你：准备好了，包括我的护照。
shī shēn qǐng biǎo shàng de mín zú guó jí xìng bié dōu tián xiě le ma
师：申请表上的民族、国籍、性别都填写了吗？
nǐ dōu tián xiě hǎo le yǒu jǐ gè kòng bái chù bù zhī dào tián shén me
你：都填写好了。有几个空白处不知道填什么。
shī xiě zhe dà shǐ guǎn guān yuán yòng de ma
师：写着"大使馆官员用"的吗？
nǐ shì de
你：是的。
shī nà yǐ xià de nǐ bú yòng tián wǒ men zěn me tōng zhī nǐ
师：那以下的你不用填。我们怎么通知你？
nǐ kě yǐ yòng shǒu jī
你：可以用手机。
shī nǐ de shǒu jī hào mǎ shì duō shǎo
师：你的手机号码是多少？
nǐ líng bā bā qī jiǔ wǔ liù sān sì yāo sì
你：零八八七九五六三四幺四。

Dialogue B

你在邮局寄一个邮包。You are in a post office, posting a parcel. Your teacher is the clerk in the post office.

shī yóu bāo jì dào shén me dì fāng
师：邮包寄到什么地方？
nǐ qiān zhèng bàn lǐ suǒ dì zhǐ zài shàng miàn
你：签证办理所，地址在上面。
shī lǐ biān shì shén me dōng xi
师：里边是什么东西？
nǐ hěn zhòng yào de zī liào wén jiàn xiàng hù zhào děng
你：很重要的资料文件，像护照等。
shī nǐ yào jì háng kōng ma
师：你要寄航空吗？
nǐ kě yǐ
你：可以。
shī nǐ yòng xìn yòng kǎ hái shì zhī piào fù qián
师：你用信用卡还是支票付钱？
nǐ xiàn jīn
你：现金。
shī zhè shì nǐ de shōu jù nǐ yào yí fèn xiáng xì de zhàng dān ma
师：这是你的收据，你要一份详细的账单吗？
nǐ bú yào le
你：不要了。

Vocabulary

dà shǐ guǎn	大使馆	embassy
guān yuán	官员	official
biǎo	表	form
tián biǎo tián xiě	填表/填写	to fill in
tián kòng	填空	to fill in a blank
hù zhào	护照	passport
qiān zhèng	签证	visa
wén jiàn	文件	document
hǎi guān	海关	(border) customs
mín zú	民族	ethnic group; nationality
guó jí	国籍	nationality
diǎn tóu	点头	to nod
dǎ zhāo hu	打招呼	to say hello; to greet
huí diàn huà	回电话	to return a phone call
huí guó	回国	to return from overseas
kòng bái chù	空白处	blank
duì huà	对话	dialogue

xìng bié	性别	gender
xiǎo tōu	小偷	thief
tōu	偷	to steal
wú suǒ wèi	无所谓	doesn't matter
fù qián	付钱	to pay
xiàn jīn xiàn qián	现金/现钱	cash
xiāng zi	箱子	case; trunk
guò lù rén	过路人	passer-by
kào jìn	靠近	close to
shuō míng	说明	to explain
jìn xíng	进行	to carry on
chá	查	to check
tōng zhī	通知	to notify
diàn huà hào mǎ	电话号码	phone number
yǐ shàng	以上	above
yǐ xià	以下	below
wèi	喂	(on phone) Hello
ruǎn jiàn	软件	software
xiāng zào	香皂	soap

sháo	勺	spoon; ladle
xìn yòng kǎ	信用卡	credit card
háng kōng	航空	aviation
jiàng luò	降落	to land
yá shuā	牙刷	toothbrush
yá gāo	牙膏	toothpaste
zhōng	钟	clock
yào shi	钥匙	key
yī guì	衣柜	wardrobe
dù jià	度假	to go on holiday
zhī piào	支票	cheque; check
shōu jù	收据	receipt
zhàng dān	账单	bill
diàn tī	电梯	elevator; lift
lóu shàng	楼上	upstairs
lóu xià	楼下	downstairs
wèi xīng diàn shì	卫星电视	satellite TV
xiū lǐ	修理	to repair
fāng gé	方格	square

Grammar

1 Generally speaking, each Chinese character has its own Pinyin (pronunciation) with one tone. When a character has more than one Pinyin and tone, it can have different meanings and functions. Here is a list of characters with more than one Pinyin, with their common compound companions:

English	Chinese	Pinyin	Attribute	English	Chinese	Pinyin	Attribute
to grow	(长)得	zhǎng	verb	long	很(长)	cháng	adjective
music	音(乐)	yuè	noun	happy	快(乐)	lè	adjective
to feel	(觉)得	jué	verb	to sleep	睡(觉)	jiào	verb
hobby	爱(好)	hào	noun/verb	good	很(好)	hǎo	adjective
teacher	(教)师	jiào	noun	to teach	(教)书	jiāo	verb
'done'	吃(了)	le	particle	to know	(了)解	liáo	verb
all/both	(都)去	dōu	adverb	capital	首(都)	dū	noun
also	(还)有	hái	adverb	to return	(还)书	huán	verb
air/vacuum	(空)调	kōng	adjective/noun	free	有(空)儿	kòng	noun
accountant	(会)计师	kuài	noun	can	也(会)	huì	verb
haircut	理(发)	fà	verb	to set off	出(发)	fā	verb
aim	目(的)	dì	noun	'possessive'	我(的)	de	particle
warm	暖(和)	huo	adjective	and	你(和)我	hé	conjunction
want	想(要)	yào	verb	demand	(要)求	yāo	verb
bank	银(行)	háng	noun	luggage	(行)李	xíng	noun
anxious	(着)急	zháo	adjective	verb +ing	走(着)	zhe	particle
quantifier	三(只)	zhī	measure word	only	(只)有	zhǐ	adverb
to plant	(种)花	zhòng	verb	type	两(种)	zhǒng	measure word

2 Four-character idioms or phrases can greatly improve any piece of writing. Here are some common and easy-to-use examples:

一般来说	generally speaking	对我来说	to me/as far as I am concerned
总而言之	in a word/in conclusion	五颜六色	colourful
各种各样	various/a variety of	男女老少	old and young, male and female
一天到晚	all day long	白天黑夜	day and night
人来人往	people coming and going	名胜古迹	ancient sites and famous places

- 对我来说一个人的身体健康最重要。To me, one's health is most important.
- 他家的男女老少都爱吃海鲜。His whole family, old and young, men and women, all like seafood.
- 街上人来人往，太热闹了。There are throngs of people in the street, so lively.

3 There are a great number of two-character words in the Chinese language. As demonstrated below, some two-character words can form new words by taking one character from each word to create a new two-character word from those characters.

Stem word	Stem word	New word
认识 (to know)	汉字 (Chinese writing)	识字 literate
自己 (self)	学习 (study/learn)	自学 self-study
农村 (countryside)	居民 (residents)	农民 (farmers/peasants)
最近 (recent)	情况 (situation)	近况 (recent situation/breaking news)
考试 (examination)	学生 (students)	考生 (exam candidates)
厨房 (kitchen)	老师 (teacher)	厨师 (chef)
相同 (same)	家乡 (hometown)	同乡 (people from the same home town)
高级 (senior)	中学 (middle school)	高中 (high school)
汽车 (car)	房子 (house)	车房 (garage)
帮助 (to help)	别人 (others)	助人 (helpful/altruistic)

Tip

Understanding characteristics of Chinese language such as this will make vocabulary learning easier.

4 Single-character words of opposing nature can also be combined to form new words.

教 (to teach)	+	学 (to learn)	=	教学 teaching/education
开 (to turn on)	+	关 (to turn off)	=	开关 switch
来 (to come)	+	去 (to go)	=	来去 journey
买 (to buy)	+	卖 (to sell)	=	买卖 trade/business
大 (big)	+	小 (small)	=	大小 size
多 (more)	+	少 (less/few)	=	多少 how much
好 (good)	+	坏 (bad)	=	好坏 quality
东 (east)	+	西 (west)	=	东西 thing

- 这个东西我没吃过，不知道好坏，多少钱一个？I have never tasted this thing before, so don't know what it is like. How much is it?
- 那个先生是做买卖的。That gentleman is in the trade business.
- 学校在大山后面，孩子每天上学来去很不容易。The school is behind the big mountain. For the children who go to school, the journey is not easy.

Practice text 24

张玉的工作是电脑软件工程师。今年她向经理申请休假一个月，到欧洲去游览。她的外文水平不错，能用流利的英语和法语进行对话。

小张的旅行箱不大，里面有几件换洗的衣服跟香皂、牙刷、牙膏、时钟等。除了钥匙和钱以外，手提包里还放了一双筷子和汤勺，没有刀叉，因为怕海关严查。

小张先在英国首都呆了一个星期，住在靠近火车站的一个旅馆里。在街上她总是跟过路人用英文打招呼，或者点点头。她呆在法国的时候买了一辆二手自行车。车坏了，她也学会了自己修理。有一天，她的钱包被小偷偷走了，不过无所谓，因为里面没有很多钱。

经理给她打了几次电话，问她什么时候回国。她回电话说明了自己继续度假的打算。她希望下一站飞机将在美国降落。

1 请阅读课文，然后选择唯一正确的答案。Read the Practice text, and then answer each question by choosing the only correct answer.

i 为什么张玉想休假一个月？
- **A** 想学外语
- **B** 想换一份工作
- **C** 想出国旅游

ii 她的钥匙放在了哪里？
- **A** 手提包里
- **B** 旅行箱里
- **C** 书包里

iii 张玉在法国使用什么交通工具
- **A** 旧自行车
- **B** 二手汽车
- **C** 走路

iv 张玉的钱包被小偷拿走了，为什么没生气？
- **A** 丢了很多钱
- **B** 丢了很少的钱
- **C** 钱包里没有钱

2 王先生跟家人刚到宾馆度假，宾馆的服务员向他们做介绍。请看图片。Mr Wang arrives at the hotel where he and his family are to spend their holiday. The hotel assistant introduces the hotel's facilities to them. Look at the pictures.

请听录音，选择五个正确的答案，表明宾馆有什么。Listen, and choose five pictures that show what the hotel has.

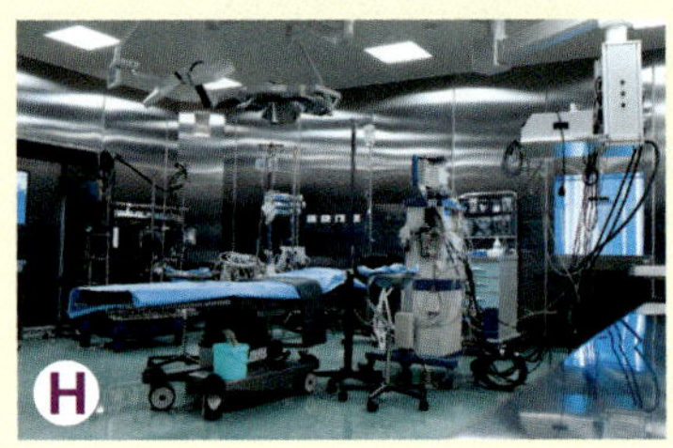

3 《学校周报》要了解一下年轻人对度假的看法，请给他们写一封150字左右的信。信里说：*School's Weekly* wants to know the opinions of young people on holidays. Write about 150 Chinese characters and say:

- 跟家人一起度假有什么好处与坏处；
- 跟朋友度假有什么好处与坏处；
- 你度假的时候喜欢跟谁在一起，为什么；
- 你觉得度假的活动怎么安排最合适。